New Panchayati Raj System
in
Bihar

New Panchayati Raj System
in
Bihar

Dr. Sheo Kumar Ram

Ankit Publications
Delhi - 110009

New Panchayati Raj System in Bihar

First Published in 2022

ISBN 978-81-950132-6-5

₹ 695

Published by : **Ankit Publications**
R-69, 3rd Floor,
Model Town-3, Delhi - 110009
Tel. : 9891553405
E-Mail: ankitapublications@gmail.com

Laser Typesetting : Aarati Computers, Delhi-110 009

Printed at : Balaji Offset, Delhi

Contents

Preface

A political subdivision constituted by law having substantial control over local affairs, including the powers to impose taxes or to extract labour for prescribed purposes, the governing body of wahich is elected can be called an institution of local self-government. Harold J. Laski has rightly observed in *Grammar of Politics* "We can not realise the full benefit of democratic government unless we begin by admission that all problems in their incidence require decision at the place and by the persons by whom the incidence most deeply felt". Decentralisation with political and administrative connonations is needed beyond doubt.

Decentralisation combined with participatory democracy constitute the basic philosophy of present Panchayat Raj System. Active participation of citizens is an essential condition for success of democracy. The creation of Panchayat Raj Institutions in India post-1973 was hailed as a step towards empowerment and development through ensured political representation secured through reservation and administration devolution.

New Panchayati Raj System faced many hiccups in Bihar. The Bihar Panchayat Raj Act 1993 that repealed the earlier Acts of 1947 and 1961 was challenged in Patna High Court which struck down certain provisions regarding reservation and judiciary at the Gram Panchayat level. This led the state government to file a special Leave Petition in the Supreme Court. The State government did not held the elections on the pretext that the matter was sub-juice. On various public interest litigations the Patna High Court observed in April 2000 that the order of the Supreme Court was being interpreted by tearing a phrase out of its context virtually by misinterpreting the Supreme Court order. The Supreme Court also clarified on 29.08.2000 that there is no bar for holding elections. Thereafter, elections could be held in 2001, in which unlike other states chairpersons' posts were not reserved for the scheduled castes and women.

The present study was conceived in 2004 in these circumstances. Elected three-tier Panchayati Raj Institutions were working and the process of devolution of funds, functions and functionaries to them were on.

In the meantime between late 2005 and early 2006, major changes occurred in the scheme. The new government enhanced reservation for women to 50% and 20% reservation was provided to extremely backward castes. It also ensured reservation on chairpersons solitary posts. Village judiciary was also constituted with the same reservation provisions.

The problem to be studied was to seek answers to the questions relating to realisation of expectations generated from the new scheme.

Following hypotheses guided the formulation of the research design.

(i) Rural Scenario of Bihar, particularly its power structure, witnessed major change due to the new PRIs

(ii) A new type of leadership, in terms of caste, class, gender, age and occupation has come at the lower levels.

(iii) Despite being elected in fair number due to

reservation, women and SCs are yet to acquire actual leadership role, they face challenge.

(iv) Devolution of functions, funds and functionaries are inadequate.

(v) Gram sabhas are yet to become a genuine mode of participatory democracy.

These bodies came only in 2001 and have undergone changes in 2006, these are still uncharted terrain in terms of academic-scholarly treatment. Though a few commentaries have appeared in newspapers and journals, systematic study has not come, while the PRIs in other states have been exhaustively studied. It is hoped that the findings of this study would prove useful to the policy planners, administrators, PRI functionaries and future researchers. The study sought to explore as to whether the increasing disenchantment with indirect democracy and increasing desire for participatory democracy engender political culture change. It sought to examine the contention of political scientists that participation makes better citizens as also the contention that decentralisation combined with democratisation may provide greater transparency, accountability, responsiveness, probity, frugality, efficiency and opportunities for mass participation.

Approach to the study was of empirically grounded field work. It focused on both ecological and structural-functional aspects of the problem. In view of the research task of testing hypotheses and seeking answer to several research questions, the study required to begin with theoretical and historical perspective. After going through the genesis, organisation and functions, process and procedures, evaluation of working of the scheme, attempts were made to accomplish the main research tasks outlined above and come to a conclusion.

Moving stepwise with the approach stated above, the methods adopted in the study were, firstly to have a critical review of theoretical-historical literature on the subject; to collect relevant data, to analyse data, interpreting and verifying results, and concluding and advancing suggestions.

The primary sources for the study were (i) interviews and questionnaires among general public;(ii) election results; (iii) detailed information as regards class, caste, gender, age and occupation of panchayat members and office bearers; (iv) proceedings of the meetings of gram sabhas, gram panchayat executives and panchayat samiti; (v) government circulars, notifications, acts, byelaws etc., (vi) Reports, proceedings and other documents of the ministries of Rural development and panchayati Raj of government of Bihar and the union government, (vii) Newspaper reports.

The secondary sources constitute the scholarly books, journal articles, seminar proceedings and studies conducted by apex institutes including National Institutes of Rural Development and United Nations Development Programme (UNDP) Decentralisation community.

The author expresses gratefulness to numerous Panchayat functionaries and others who generously cooperated during operationalisation of questionnaires and interviews. The author immensely benefited from the material provided by several websites of the government of India, UNDP and many others. He must particularly mention the cooperation extended by R.C.P. Yadav (Mukhia) and Suresh Ram (Pramukh of Paroo).

Gratefulness has also to be acknowledged to the University Grants Commission (UGC) New Delhi and its Kolkata based Eastern Regional Centre.

In so far as the completion of the work is concerned, the author is deeply indebted to Dr. Anil Kumar Ojha of the University Department of Political Science, B. R. A. University Muzaffarpur, for his pains and patience through the work. He has to express his gratefulness to Dr. K.C. Chandhary and Dr. R. N. Kumar former Heads of the Departments, for their encouragements. He would be failing in his duty if does not express gratitude to the present Head of the University Department, Professor Nagendra Prasad Chaudhary, who during his tenure as the Principal of SRPS College Jaintpur. He is also grateful to learned teachers at the University Department of Political Science—Professor R. Dubey, Dr, U. Mishra, CCDC; Dr. Naresh Kumar, Dr. C. D. Amar, Dr. Anjana Jha and Dr. B. K. Rai and also to Dr. Kumari Saroj of M.D.D.M College, Muzaffarpur, his Senior Colleagues Dr. T.C. Sharma and Prof. Ashok at S.R.P.S College, for their sympathies.

The fond memories of author's father late Muneshwar Ram and mother late Yashoda Devi remained a source of inspiration. The good wishes of his wife Neelam Kumari also contributed.

- Dr. Sheo Kumar Ram

1

Introduction

This introductory chapter begins with the discussion on the concept of decentralisation in democratic governance as it has evolved in India. Then, it focuses on significant landmarks in the progress of Indian Panchayati Raj System, particularly with reference to Bihar.

I. The Concept of Local Self- Government and Panchayats

Panchayati Raj is an ancient institution with a new concept. The modern states with multitudinous activities and an all-pervasive concern in each branch of life, threaten the society with the danger of monolithism. The governments' activity is necessarily impersonal. Against its rather abstract view, there is a perpetual rebellion. At this point, the reasoned claim for local government takes form. Said Laski in his *The Grammar of Politics*—we cannot realise the full benefit of democratic government unless we begin by admission that all problems in their incidence require decision at the place, and by the persons by whom the incidence most deeply felt.[1] From this emerges the need for decentralisation with political and administrative connotations—constituting a centrifugal movement.

So far as the concept of Panchayati Raj is concerned, it

is the contemporary pluralist tradition in democratic theory that provides theoretical base to it. According to Frank Cunningham, a small participatory community in which every citizen plays a role in political decision-making is considered an example of most democratic situation.[2]

In such a situation, decisions are made by all members of a society. All are considered rational and well-informed. Village panchayats are supposed to be a community where the common good is decided by consensus or majority vote after full debate.

Contemporary communitarian theorist Robert Putnam enumerates three conditions for the success of democracy:

(a) active participation of citizens in public affairs,

(b) the interaction of citizens as equals, and

(c) mutual trust and respect among citizens.[3]

Putnam stresses on creation of social capital; social capital means mutual trust and commitment to common projects necessary for democratically coordinated activity. Putnam underlines that a democracy is at its most robust from when there is energetic citizens' participation in taking collective action.

The term participatory democracy was coined by Arnold Kaufman in 1960.[4] However, theorists have pointed out that the deliberative democratic practices are only appropriate among those who are prepared to reason together in the right spirit.

While the ubiquitous phenomenon of concentration of power has been explained by theorists, there have been consistent suggestions for division and dispersal of power. The benefits of democratic decentralisation are elaborated by Richard Crook and James Manor as, "Decentralisation combined with democratisation might provide greater transparency, accountability, responsiveness, probity, frugality, efficiency, equity and opportunities for mass participation..."[5]

The United Nations Division of Public Administration defines a local government as 'a political subdivision of a nation (or, in a federal system, a State) which is constituted by law and has substantial control of local affairs, including the powers to impose taxes or to extract labour for prescribed purposes. The governing body of such an entity is elected or otherwise locally selected...'[6]

Hugh Whalen adds that 'each unit of local government in any system is assumed to possess the following characteristics: a given territory and population, an institutional structure...a separate legal entity, a range of powers and functions authorised by delegation from appropriate central or intermediate legislature and lastly within the ambit of such a delegation, subject always... to the test of reasonableness'.[7]

Panchayats Since Ancient Times in India

The institution of Panchayat has existed in India since ancient times. The term "Panchayat" literally means a council of five. The principle of the panchayat is "Panch Parmeshwar", which means 'God Speaking through the five'. The village was an autonomous republic and its affairs were governed by the Panchayats. It was usually a democratically constituted body as its members were chosen by the people. Its members being the elders of the village community, commanded respect and their decisions were obeyed. The villagers led a corporate life and the Panchayats not only looked after their needs but also settled their disputes, legal as well as social. It functioned through committees which looked after different aspects of rural life, such as, the maintenance of water tanks and gardens, and enforcement of law and order. The life practically remained undisturbed by the political changes. Will Durant, the American thinker and historian, writes, "The village community in ancient India —panchayat system— is the proto-type of all forms of self government and democracy that have ever been evolved in various parts of the world"[8].

One generalization that has been made regarding local self government in ancient times is that it was far more successful than in the days of British rule or even at present. It was far more widespread because as has been brought out by historical research almost every village in the country had in ancient times a self-governing body of its own. It was all the more the case in the past. And if every village had then a self-governing body it meant that almost all people enjoyed the advantages of local self-government.

In contrast to this it was only a small percentage of villages that had Panchayats in the days of British rule and it is only after the country became independent that attempts were made to have Panchayats in every village or groups of villages. It is because of this that we are entitled to say that local self-government was more widespread in ancient India, a truth which is usually conveyed by the statement the pre-British India was a land of village republics.[9]

During the medieval period, the Muslim rulers did not interfere with the working of the Panchayats, they simply ignored their existence. As such, during the Muslim period the Panchayats deteriorated considerably. But the East India Company and the British were largely responsible for the decay of these self-governing institutions. The new system of land tenure which recognised only the individual, the rapid means of transport and communication which ended the political isolation and economic self sufficiency of the villages, and the centralised system of administration had contributed to the decline of the Panchayats with the shake up of the country. Political and economic foundations, the social structure began to show signs of disintegration. The social and economic ties built up through the ages by the Panchayats were broken, the Panchayat themselves also degenerated. Instead of being agencies of social good, they become instruments of exploitation in the hands of rich and influential people.

Gandhi's Views on Panchayats

Mahatma Gandhi, who identified Panchayati Raj with *Ram Rajya,* says that just as *Ram* was the ruler servant of Ayodhya, so was the sarpanch is the ruler-servant of the village. As such, Gandhi always advocated the introduction of gram Swaraj or village republic. He said, "My idea of village Swaraj is that it is a complete republic, independent of its neighbours for its own vital wants, and yet interdependent for many others in which dependence is a necessity."[10]

He wrote in *Harijan* that Indian independence must begin at the bottom. Thus every village will be a republic Panchayat having full powers. In this structure, composed of innumerable villages there will be ever widening never descending circles. It is for this reason that some people believe that Panchayats are *Panch Mukh Parmeshwar*.

Mahatma Gandhi said, "My idea of village Swaraj is that it is a complete republic independent of its neighbours for its own vital wants, and yet interdependent for many others in which dependence is a necessity. Thus every village's first concern will to grow its own food crops and cotton for its cloth. It should have a reserve for its cattle, recreation and playground for adults and children. Then if there is more land available, it will grow useful money crops, thus excluding ganja, tobacco, opium and the like. The village will maintain a village theatre, school and public hall. It will have its own waterworks ensuring clean water supply. This can be done through controlled wells or tanks. Education will be compulsory up to the final basic course. As far as possible every activity will be conducted on the co-operative basis. There will be no caste such as we have today with their graded untouchability. Non-violence with the techniques of *Satyagraha* and non-cooperation will be the sanction of village community. There will be a compulsory service of village guards who will be selected by the village. The government of the village will be conducted by the Panchayat of five persons annually elected by the adult villagers, male and female, possessing minimum prescribed qualifications. These will have all the authority and jurisdiction required since there will be no system of punishments in the accepted sense. This Panchayat will be the legislature, judiciary and executive confined to operate for its year of office. Any village can become such a republic today without much interference even from the present government whose sole effective connection with the villages is the execution of the village revenue. I have not examined here the question of relations with the neighbouring villages and the centre if any. My purpose is to present an outline of village government. Here there is perfect democracy based upon individual freedom. The individual is the architect of his own government. The law of non-violence rules him and his government. He and his village are able to defy the might of a world. For the law governing every villager is that he will suffer death in the defence of his and his village's honour"[11].

II. Important Evolutionary Landmarks

India was having formal elective local bodies during British period also. However, the Corporation of Madras (1688) was the first such modern body. British rule in India passed through two phases.

In the first phase, which ended in 1858, government was carried out by the East India Company when Municipal Corporations were established in the presidency towns of Calcutta, Madras and Bombay. Local Magistrates had set up informal committees here and there to collect funds for being spent on conservancy, police and roads. It was only in 1842 that the first statute was passed to provide for municipal committees, which was replaced by another Act in 1850. One feature of both these is that people of the town were expected to take the initiative in setting up a municipal body and this proved to be one of the causes of their failure.

The second phase of India under the British Crown saw major advancements including Samuel Laing's Financial Statement,1861-62; Lord Mayo's Resolution on Provincial Finance, 1870; Lord Ripon's Resolution on Local Self-Government,1882; recommendations of the Royal Commission on Decentralisation,1909; Montagu-Chelmsford Report on Local self-Government, 1918; and reconstruction of Local Self-Government during Provincial Autonomy. The Bihar and Orrisa Municipal and District Board Acts of 1922 and Bihar Panchayati Raj Act 1947 were the major land marks of pre-Constitution advancements.

Though local government institutions have existed in India since ancient times, but these could acquire formal representative character during the British Period. British rule in India passed through two stages.

Pre-1858

In the first phase beginning from 1687 a municipal corporation was set up in 1687 at Madras, on the pattern of English borough. The underlying idea was that the people would tax themselves and thus, relieve the East India Company of having heavy taxes on the people. But the people opposed the taxation proposal and so in 1726, the corporation was abolished and in its place a mayor's court was established which had primarily judicial functions. Governor-General and Governors appointed by the East India Company spent all their time on war and conquest and consolidation of the territories conquered. They showed little or no interest in the promotion of civic or national welfare except in the Presidency towns of Madras, Bombay and Calcutta where municipal corporations were established under the Charter Act of 1793. The Act authorised the Governor-General to appoint Justices of the Peace in these towns, who were empowered to levy taxes on lands and houses, and to provide for maintenance of roads, scavenging and police.

In fact, the governmental system in India had become highly centralised under the Act of 1833. It was only gradually that the evils arising from it became clear. The Bengal Act of 1842 extended to the district towns in Bengal the power to set up town committees for sanitary purposes upon application made by two-thirds of the house-holders in the town. Since the Act empowered the committee to impose direct taxes, the people did not appreciate the idea and no town come forward for the establishment of a town committee for it[12]. In 1850, an Act was passed for the entire country repealing the 1842 Act[13]; it also met with failure because of the reluctance of the people of self-taxation.

Post-1858

Since towns were not coming forward voluntarily for the establishment of town committees, a series of acts were passed after 1863 which authorised provincial governments to establish municipal governments and entrust them the functions relating to lighting, sanitation and water supply.

The year 1870 witnessed Lord Mayo's famous resolution which provided for further decentralization from the centre to the provinces, emphasized the desirability of associating Indians in administration, and indicated the best way of doing it was to have municipal government. The resolution read, "The operation of this resolution, in its meaning and integrity, will afford opportunities for the development of Self-Government, for strengthening Municipal Institutions, and for the association of Natives and Europeans to a greater extent than heretofore, in the administration of affairs[14]. Mayo's Resolution led to the first great step in local self-government not only in urban but also in rural areas. It is this that gives significance to this Resolution in the evolution of local-self government in India.

It is significant to note that the first phase of evolution of these bodies really extends up to 1881, during which the British government instituted the system of Local Government to give relief to the central exchequer. Further, in order to have dominant position, the British had packed these local bodies with nominated members who toed the British line. The Local people have very little say in the matter.

Lord Ripon's Initiatives

Samuel Laing's Financial Statement, 1861-62 and Lord Mayo's Resolution on Provincial Finance, 1870 could not be counted as real advancement in terms of evolution of decentralised governance involving Indians. The real second phase in the evolution of local government in India begins in 1882 with the arrival of Lord Ripon, who succeeded Lord Mayo.

Lord Ripon is rightly regarded as the father of local-self government in modern India. By the time he became the Viceroy, the first generation of educated Indians inspired by the ideals of democracy and liberty emerged and they demanded a share in the government of the country. As a liberal, it was not possible for Lord Ripon to ignore such a demand. At the same time, he felt that the time is not yet ripe for giving them a share in central or provincial government and they should be first trained in the sphere of local government. A man of liberal outlook, he resolved to make local government self-governing. He considered these institutions as instruments of popular and political education. He also believed that as education advanced there is rapidly growing up all over the country an intelligent class of public-spirited men whom it is not only bad policy, but sheer waste of power to fail to utilise. Moreover, it would shift some of the ever-growing burden of administration to local authorities.

Lord Ripon's resolution said that local bodies should be elected and should have non-governmental members and

Chairman. It is a comprehensive resolution and deals with administrative areas, the constitution of local bodies, their functions, finances and powers.[15]

This Resolution led to the passing of acts in different provinces for establishing local government. The Resolutions issued by Government of India in subsequent years did not embody any new principle not found in that of Ripon but only carried a step to further their practical application. It is thus the most important landmark in the evolution of local self-government in modern India. However, in many provinces the government did not interpret the Resolution liberally and so much of its purpose was defeated. In the meantime, reviews of municipal administration was undertaken in 1896 and that of Local Boards in 1897.

The Royal Commission on Decentralisation (1909)[16] for the first time put forward a powerful plea for the resuscitation of the village. Immediate effect was not given to its recommendation on this subject; attempts were made from this time on to establish informal village authorities. Though the Village was the basic unit of local self-government in ancient and medieval times, its importance was completely ignored in the scheme of local self-government organised by the British till then.

It suggested that Village should be regarded as a basic unit of local self-government and every village should have a Panchayat. The Royal Commission also recommended the devolution of more powers on *Taluk* or Sub-district Boards. It said that the majority of members of local bodies should be elected. They should be entrusted with more functions. Their power of taxation should be increased. The municipality should elect its own chairman, but the collector should continue to be chairman of District Board. However, practically nothing could be done because of outbreak of the First World War in 1914.

At the end of the war, government of India issued a

resolution which more or less repeated the resolution of the Royal Commission of 1909. For instance, it said that Panchayats should be revived in villages, the president of the local body should be an elected person, and local bodies should have full freedom in the preparation of budget, imposition of taxes and sanction of public works.

The Government of India Act of 1919 proved to be a turning point in the field of local government. It had begun a new phase in the evolution of local government. Due to the assistance given by India to Britain in the war, and the growing national movement compelled the British to announce increasing association of Indians in every branch of the administration with a view to progressive realisation of home rule in India. The practice of having an official as the chairman of a local body practically disappeared, the right to vote was liberalised; the local bodies were given more powers in financial matters and in the executive field. Eminent persons like Pandit Jawaharlal Nehru, Sardar Vallabh Bhai Patel and Pursottam Das Tandon entered municipal councils to work these institutions.

However, some commentators observe that due to lack of education, civic sense, and experience in managing our own affairs, this democratic venture did not make much headway. The democratisation of local government brought about inefficiency in the administration of local affairs. Corruption and favouritism increased. The local politicians became very influential and as such Local Civil Service began to work for their interest rather than for the common good.[17] Politicisation of these bodies surfaced. Its glaring example was suppression of Gaya District Board in Bihar in early 1929. Its chairman and a prominent Congress leader Anugraha Narain Sinha narrates in his autobiography that he was having a political rivalry with the supporters of Sir Ganesh Dutt Singh, the then provincial minister from 1923 to 1935-36 of local self-government under dyarchy, that led to his ouster[18]. Legendary peasant leader, Swami Sahajanand states that even an explanation was not asked from Sinha.[19]

A thorough analysis of the functioning of local government was made by the Simon Commission in 1930. However, the system continued until the enforcement of the provincial part of the Government of India Act 1935 in 1937.

A new phase of evolution of local government begins with the coming into force of the Government of India Act of 1935 in the provinces which established provincial autonomy. The administration of local government was now fully in the hands of ministers. This led to the democratisation of local bodies by the abolition of nominations and the separation of deliberative functions from the executive ones.

Debates in the Constituent Assembly on the Indian Village, 1949

The debates in the constituent assembly on the importance of the village in the political life of the country reveal the existence of two conflicting ideas among political leaders. There were those who took a romantic view of the village in ancient India and who wanted it to play the same part in the future political set-up of the country as it did in the past. They showed a tendency to ignore how the community spirit in the village was completely disintegrated under the influence modernisation in the course of the last two centuries. Even a great admirer of the village community like Mr. Jaya Prakash Narayan observed: "The old village communities have survived in nothing else than their physical existence. They are no longer living communities acting jointly for the solution of individual or communal problems and for material life"[20].

Opposed to the romanticists were leaders like Dr. Bhim Rao Ambedkar who had nothing but contempt for Indian villages. During the course of his speech while initiating the debate Dr. Ambedkar made a reference to the Indian villages as under:

"Another criticism against the Draft Constitution is that no part of it represents the ancient polity of India. It is said that the new Constitution should have been drafted on the entire ancient Hindu model of a State and that instead of incorporating Western theories the new constitution should have been raised and built upon village Panchayats and district Panchayats. There are others who have taken a more extreme view. They do not want any central or provincial governments. They just want India to contain so many village governments. The love of the intellectual Indians for the village community is of course infinite if not pathetic. It is largely due to the fulsome praise bestowed upon it by Metcalfe who described them as little republics having nearly everything that they want within themselves, and almost independent of any foreign relations. The existence of these village communities each one forming a separate little State in itself has according to Metcalfe contributed more than any other cause to the preservation of the people of India, through all the revolutions and changes which they have suffered, and is in a high degree conducive to their happiness and to the enjoyment of a great portion of the freedom and independence. No doubt the village communities have lasted where nothing else lasts. But those who take pride in the village communities do not care to consider what little part they have played in the affairs and the destiny of the country; and why ? Their part in the destiny of the country has been well described by Metcalfe himself who says:

"Dynasty after dynasty tumbles down. Revolution succeeds do revolution. Hindoo, Pathan, Mogul, Mahratha, Sikh, English are all masters in turn but the village communities remain the same. In times of trouble they arm and fortify themselves. A hostile army passes through the country. The village

> communities collect their cattle within their walls, and let the enemy pass unprovoked."
>
> Such is the part the village communities have played in the history of their country. Knowing this, what pride can one feel in them? That they have survived through all vicissitudes may be a fact. But mere survival has no value. The question is on what plane they have survived, surely on a low, on a selfish level. I hold that these village republics have been the ruination of India. I am, therefore, surprised that those who condemn provincialism and communalism should come forward as champions of the village. What is the village but a sink of localism, a den of ignorance, narrow-mindedness and communalism? I am glad that the Draft Constitution has discarded the village and adopted the individual as its units[21].

Member after member who followed Dr. Ambedkar rose to express their sorrow, resentment, and disappointment at his provoking reference to Village India. Though most of the members, who participated in the debate, criticised Dr. Ambedkar for not giving any importance or place to the village in the Constitution, members like Pandit Balkrishna Sharma and Alladi Krishnaswami Ayyar pointed out in their speeches that there was nothing to prevent the provincial legislature from constituting the villages as administrative units.

Some of the important speeches are given below, as briefly as possible, to indicate how much importance was attached to the villages and village Panchayats by prominent Indian leaders in their statements made during the debate in the Constituent Assembly, when the subject was under discussion.

Mr. H. V. Kamath (C.P. and Berar):

> "On one thing I join issue with Dr. Ambedkar. He was pleased to refer to the village – I am quoting from a

press report in the absence of the official copy – as 'sinks of localism and dens of ignorance, narrow-mindedness and communalism'; and he also laid at the door of a certain Metcalfe our 'pathetic faith' in village communities. I may say that it is not owing to Metcalfe but owing to a far greater man who has liberated us in recent times, our Master and the Father of our nation, that this love of ours for the villages has grown, our faith in the village republics and our rural communities has grown and we have cherished it with all our heart. It is due to Mahatma Gandhi that we have come to love our village folk. With all deference to Dr. Ambedkar, I differ from him in this regard. His attitude yesterday was typical of the urban highbrow; and if that is going to be our attitude towards the village folk, I can only say, 'God Save us'. If we do not cultivate sympathy and love and affection for our villages and rural folk, I do not see how we can uplift our country. Mahatma Gandhi taught us in almost the last *mantra* that he gave in the best days of his life to strive for Panchayati Raj. If Dr. Ambedkar cannot see his way to accept this, I do not see what remedy or panacea he has got for uplifting our villages. In my own province of C. P. and Berar we have recently launched upon a scheme of *Janapadas*, of local self-government and decentralization; and that is entirely in consonance with the teachings of our Master. I hope that scheme will come to fruition and be an example to the rest of the country. It was with considerable pain that I heard Dr. Ambedkar refer to our villages in that fashion, with dislike, if not with contempt."[22]

Mr. T. Prakasam (Madras):

"So far as the drafting of this constitution is concerned, with all respect to Dr. Ambedkar, I must say that he has not been able to put himself in the position of those who had been fighting for the freedom of this country for thirty long years. In one stroke, he condemned the village panchayats system. He has referred to the remarks of one great man of those old days of the British, Mr. Metcalfe, and the description given by him that the village panchayats existed and continued, whatever may have been happening with regard to the government at the top; whoever may have come and whoever may have gone, they did not concern themselves. It is not a matter which should have been treated by Dr. Ambedkar in that manner. That was a condition to which we had been reduced after the village panchayats had been exhausted on account of the oppression of the various foreign rulers who had come over to this country. Still in spite of all that had been done for their suppression, they had survived. That is what Metcalfe wanted to explain to the world and to us who had been ignoring it. Therefore, village panchayat is not to be condemned on that basis. I do not advocate for one moment today that village Panchayat should be such as described by Metcalfe under those circumstances. Village panchayat should be one which is up-to-date, which gives real power to rule and to get money and expend it, in the hands of the villagers."[23]

Mr. Alladi Krishnaswami Ayyar (Madras):

(One of the criticisms had been that) "...the Constitution does not give sufficient importance to village communities which are an essential feature of India's social and political life. With the large powers vested in the provincial or State legislatures in regard to local self-government and other matters, there is nothing to prevent the provincial legislatures, from constituting the villages as administrative units for the discharge of various functions vested in the state Governments."[24]

Prof. N. G. Ranga (Madras):

"I am most unhappy that Dr. Ambedkar should have said what he has said about the village panchayats. All the democratic tradition of our country has been lost on him. If he had only known the achievements of the village panchayats in Southern India over a period of millennium, he certainly would not have said those things. If he had cared to study the Indian history with as much care as he seems to have devoted to the history of other countries, he certainly would not have ventured those remarks. I wish to remind the House of the necessity for providing as many political institutions as possible in order to enable our villagers to gain as much experience in democratic institutions in order to be able to discharge their responsibilities through adult suffrage in the new democracy that we are going to establish. Without this foundation-stone of village panchayats in our country, how would it be possible for our masses to play their rightful part in our democracy? Do we want centralisation of administration or decentralisation? Mahatma Gandhi has pleaded over a period of thirty years for decentralisation. We as Congressmen are committed to decentralisation. Indeed all the world is today in favour of decentralisation."[25]

Mr. M. Ananthasayanam Ayyangar:

"As we are situated today, is it at all possible immediately to base our constitution on village republics? I agree this ought to be our objective. But where are these republics? They have to be brought into existence. Therefore, I would advise that in the directives, a clause must be added, which would insist upon the various Governments that may come into existence in future to establish village Panchayats, give them political autonomy and also economic independence in their own way to manage their own affairs."[26]

Mr. Mahavir Tyagi (U.P.):

"Then, a word about the villages, Dr. Ambedkar said that he was happy that the 'Drafting committee has not accommodated the village'. He characterised it as 'a sink of localism and a den of communalism'. It is these sinks of slavery that were facing all sorts of repression in the freedom struggle. When these sinks of slavery those were being charred, burnt and tortured in Chimoor, the pyramids of freedoms were applying grease on the back of the Britishers. Unless I raise my voice against the remarks which Dr. Ambedkar has made against villages, I cannot face my village people. Dr. Ambedkar does not know what amount of sacrifice the villagers have undergone in the struggle for freedom. I submit that villagers should be given their due share in the governance of the country."[27]

Mr. N. Madhava Rau (Mysore):

"For over thirty years, the Mysore Government have put the revival of village communities and the improvement of the working of village panchayats in the forefront of their activities. A great deal of public expenditure has been incurred on this account. All officers concerned from the Dewan to the Tahsildar have, according to their lights, given personal attention to the condition of the villages. The present popular government in Mysore are, I understand, making still more intensified efforts in the same direction. The results are, in my opinion, encouraging and in some cases quite gratifying. It is true, some villages are chronically faction-ridden and indulge in petty tyrannies, or remain the strongholds of untouchability. A considerable number are pathetic or even moribund. But, about 30 per cent could be

> classed as good, that is to say, they had held regular meetings, collected panchayat taxes, undertaken some optional duties and carried out works of public utility and weekly cleaning by voluntary labour contributed by the villagers and had taken steps to ensure the vaccination of children and so on. The success that has been achieved such as it is, is largely conditioned by the initiative of a good headman or other influential land-lord. I am sure that experience in other parts of the country is more or less the same."[28]

So, it is clear from the Constituent Assembly Debates that the founding fathers sharply differed—the Gandhians were stressing on according constitutional status to Panchayats, while constitutionalists were sceptical. That is why its institutionalisation was left to be done later. It was put as a Directive Principle of the State Policy and as a subject of legislation it was placed in the State List.

Last Phase: Evolution Since Independence

But a marked change took place with the dawn of Indian Independence. There was self-government not only at the local level, but also at provincial and central levels. In 1948, a conference of local government ministers from all over India met at Delhi under the chairmanship of the central minister of Health to exchange ideas with regard to various problems facing local authorities. It was inaugurated by Prime Minister Pt. Jawaharlal Nehru, who characterised these as grass roots of democracy and a factor for national integration. He said in his speech, "Local self government is and must be the basis of any true system of democracy. We have got rather into the habit of thinking of democracy at the top and not so much below. Democracy at the top may not be a success unless you build on this foundation from below."[29]

In Bihar after independence, Bihar Panchayati Raj Act 1947 was passed. It was enacted as Bihar Act (VII) of 1948 and came into force in 1949[30].

The dawn of independence lent new urgency to the movement for popularising the Panchayats. The post-independence era was marked by several developments in this field. Gandhian philosophy of ruralism, the Constitution of India, the five-year plans, and community development movement were at work in it. The makers' of the Indian Constitution stressed the need to revitalize and rehabilitate them.

Constitutional Scheme at the dawn of Independence— The last phase of evolution begins in 1950 with the Constitution of India coming into operation, which has made local government a State subject as entry 5 of State list under seventh schedule and as Directive Principles of State Policy at Article 40 under Part IV, which reads as, "The state shall take steps to organise village Panchayats and endow them with such powers and authority as may be necessary to enable them to function as units of self-government". Further, Entry 5 of the State List under Seventh Schedule reads as, "Local Government, that is to say, the constitution and powers of municipal corporations, improvement trusts, district boards, mining settlement authorities and other local authorities for the purpose of local self-government or village administration".

Community Development Programme

Community Development Programme (CDP) was launched on October 2, 1952 initially in 55 Pilot Projects which was to cover the whole country later on. It sought to achieve all-round development through efforts of the beneficiaries themselves. It followed an integrative approach to the village community.

The Sarvodaya School of Shantineketan (Bengal) 1921, the Marthandom experiment (old Travancore-Cochin State) 1921, the experiment at Gurgaon (Punjab) 1927, the experiment in Baroda state in 1932, the Firka development Scheme in Maharashtra (1948) and the Etawah Project, in

U.P. (1948) has taught many lessons and that accumulated experience helped in formulating the strategy of the programmes.

The objectives of the CDP were: "First increase employment and increase production by the application of scientific methods of agriculture including horticulture, animal husbandry, fisheries etc. and the establishment of subsidiary and cottage industries, secondly, self-help and self reliance and the largest public extension of the principle of co-operation and thirdly, the need for developing a portion of the vast unutilised time and energy in the countryside for the benefit of the community"[31].

The various programme of CDP to attain its objectives were carried out through the government departments. The bureaucracy has certain in-built structural limitations which do not provide initiative to the beneficiaries. The local community was receiving programmes without much involvement of its own in formulating them. These were carried out with government participation rather than people's participation. Democratic decentralisation differs from de-concentration, devolution, and delegation. Balwantrai Mehta Committee report— The study team on Community Projects and National Extension Service appointed by the Government of India in 1957 commonly known as Balwantrai Mehta Committee said, "It is not infrequently that delegation of power is mistaken for decentralisation. The former does not divest the government of the ultimate responsibility for the actions of the authority to whom power is delegated; this authority is under the control of the government and is in every way subordinate to it. Decentralisation, on the other hand, is a process whereby the government divests itself completely of certain duties and responsibilities and devolves them on certain other authority."[32]

The committee on Plan Project (Balwantrai Mehta) remarked in 1957. "So long as we do not discover or create a representative and democratic institution which will be supplementing the local interest supervision and care necessary to ensure that expenditure of money upon local objects conforms with the needs and wishes of the locality invest in with adequate power and assign to it appropriate finances, we assign to it appropriate finances, we will never be able to evoke local interest and excite local initiative in the field of development."

However with all its vitality, institutional structure, built in methods of administration, the C.D.P. was found wanting. It was losing its 'extension'. Content and its 'methods', elements were making the system more rigid, centralized, expenditure biased and was concentrating on 'physical outputs' as against 'non-physical' outputs which ultimately sustain and increase the major capital stock of an industrial nation. Its physical particularly economic results were also not equal to the expectations of the planners. The fifth development commissioner's conference in May, 1956 had observed: "We can not go far from where we have arrived unless we have a wider partnership with technical department, wider partnership with people's institutions and wider partnership with political institutions of the country."

The C.D.P. was basically a method described as the extension approach. It was a means category concept, if not an end itself as some believed. As a method it was not extraneous to Panchayati Raj.

The spirit of C.D.P. was sought to be nourished later on with popular support and participation within the fold of Panchayati Raj after the adoption of Balwantrai Mehta Committee report.

The development of Panchayati Raj, therefore, can be said to be the logical outcome of the community development Programme. Panchayati Raj, as described by Harrison as the most important potential invention of Independent India, is a complex system of rural self-government. Panchayati

Raj, a new phase of local government was ushered in by democratic decentralisation to make the lower units of administration more popularly elected, more socially broad-based and more engaged in wider range of activities than hitherto.

Panchayati Raj is regarded as the heart and soul of Indian politics. The health and strength of Indian democracy depends on its sound functioning. It is the agency of social progress, economic and political development. The objectives of Panchayati Raj are decentralization development, social change and institutional leadership under its aegis forms the nucleus of new emerging elite in rural India.

Conceptually, local government is multi-dimensional, an integrant of the political mechanism for governance. With the emergence of development as the goal of humanity, Indian rural local government units have come to perform four-fold development functions—promotion of popular participation, spurring of economic development, social transformation and equitable distribution.

Panchayati Raj has passed through four distinct phases within its short span of life:

The Phase of Ascendency

The period from 1959 to 1964 was described as the phase of ascendancy. It witnessed important landmarks in the history of Panchayat Raj. The basic pillars of the Panchayati Raj structure were erected in a constructive and future oriented style during this period. This period witnessed the appointment of Balwantrai Mehta Committee.

Balwantrai Mehta Committee was appointed in 1956 to study the whole problem and suggest ways and means for implementing the scheme of Panchayati Raj on some uniform lines throughout the country. On 12 January 1958 the National Development Council endorsed its recommendations. Therefore, the central council of the Local Self-government at its fifth meeting held at Hyderabad in 1959 took stock of the action taken by the states to implement the decision of the NDC. At this stage it recommended, "While the broad pattern and fundamentals may be uniform there should not be any rigidity in the pattern. In fact the country is so large and Panchayati Raj is so consequences that there is the fullest scope of trying out various patterns and alternatives. What is most important is genuine transfer of power to the people, if this is ensured. Forms and pattern may necessarily vary according to the conditions prevailing in different states."

The Balwantrai Mehta Committee made the following important recommendations:

1. The government should divest itself completely of certain duties and responsibilities and devolve them to these bodies which will have the entire charge of all development work within its Jurisdiction, reserving to itself only the functions of guidance supervision and higher planning.
2. At the block level an elected self-governing institution should be set up with its jurisdiction co-existing with a development block.
3. The Panchayati Samiti should be constituted by indirect election from the village Panchayats.
4. The functions of Panchayat Samiti should cover the development of agriculture in all its aspects, improvement of administration of Primary Schools, and collections and maintenance of statistics. It should also act as an agent of state government in executing special schemes of development entrusted to it. Other functions should be transferred to the Panchayat Samiti only when they have started functioning as efficient democratic institutions.
5. The state government should give to those Samiti

adequate grants-in-aid conditionally or unconditionally or on matching basis with regard to economically backward areas.

6. All central and state funds spent in a block areas should invariably be assigned to the Panchayat Samiti to be spent directly or indirectly excepting when the Samiti recommended direct assistance to institutions.

7. A certain amount of control should inevitably be retained by government e.g., the power of superseding a Panchayat Samiti in public interest.

8. The condition of the Panchayati should purely be on a elective basis with the provision for co-operation of two women members and one member each from the scheduled castes and scheduled tribes. No other special groups need to be given special representation.

9. Main resources of income of Panchayat will be property of house tax, tax on markets and vehicles, Octori or terminal tax conservancy tax, water and lighting rates, income from cattle ponds, grants from Panchayat Samiti and fees charged from the registration of animals sold.

10. The budget of the village Panchayat will be subjected to scrutiny and approval of the Panchayat Samiti, chief officer of which will exercise the same power in regard to the village Panchayat as the collector will in regard to the Zila Parishad. No village Panchayat should, however, be superseded except by the state government who will do so only on the recommendation of the Zila Parishad.

11. The compulsory duties of the village Panchayats should include among others provision of water supply, sanitation, lighting maintenance of roads, land, management, collection and maintenance of records and other statistics and the welfare of back

ward classes. It will also act as an agent of the Panchayati Samiti in executing any scheme entrusted to it.

12. The Judicial Panchayat may have much large Jurisdiction than even a gram sevak's circle, and out of the panel suggested by village Panchayats the sub-divisional or direct magistrate may select persons to from judicial Panchayat.
13. To ensure necessary co-ordination between the Panchayat Samiti, a Zila Parishad should be constituted consisting of the Presidents of these Samitis, MLAs and MPs representing the area and the district level officers. The collector will be its Chairman and one of his officers will act as Secretary.

Undoubtedly, the Balwantrai Mehta Committee was confronted with the problem of how to lay down some uniform lines of Panchayati Raj in view of the vast size and varying social, political and economic conditions prevailing in different parts of the country. It was thus properly visualised by the Balwantrai Mehta Committee and wisely endorsed by the National Development Council to take into view board patterns of the scheme without sticking the idea of a rigid uniformity that would have made their job not only tedious but impossible as well. As a result the government of India did not insist that every state should follow the same pattern. The second phase between 1965 and 1969 was described as the phase of stagnation. During this period no serious attempts or efforts were made to revamp or to revitalise the Panchayati Raj has been in a low profile. As a form of Local government, it has fallen out of favour everywhere except in Maharashtra and in Gujarat, where it has been relatively more successful. Increasingly its justification is sought purely in terms of an agency to augment agricultural production.

The stagnation is the result to four major factors. The

new national and state level leadership which emerged around 1966 had much thinner links with the ideals of Mahatma Gandhi and thus much weaker ideological commitment to Panchayat Raj. Secondly, the mounting food shortage of this period and the crop failures of 1966-67 led to a reshuffling of priorities in the community development programme itself, resulting in an over-riding emphasis on agricultural production. In the process a comprehensive concept of internal development got the process a major project for agricultural production.

Thirdly, the trend of Indian Political System has been markedly centralized since the mid-sixties but the pace towards centralisation of power got considerably accelerated since 1960's. During that Period Political leadership, the State government were being made subservient to the central government. This exactly is not the climate under which Panchayati Raj can grow and flourish.

Fourthly, the technology discovered this time served only to reinforce the already powerful centralised pressure, in the process, relegating Panchayati Raj to a lower, even unimportant status.

The Phase of Decline (1969-1983)

The third phase in the history of the Panchayati Raj is the period between 1969 and 1983. This was a period of decline. No serious or sincere effort was made either at the centre or at the state level like the period of stagnation as mentioned above. In the political side, the phase witnessed the change of the congress ministry at the centre and it culminated in the appointment of Ashoka Mehta Committee in 1977 to revamp the Panchayati Raj Structure. As far as the state were concerned Karnataka, West Bengal, Andhra Pradesh made appreciable efforts to rejuvenate the Panchayati Raj structure in their areas.

Ashoka Mehta Committee submitted its report in 1978.

The major recommendations of the committee were:

1. In the Panchayati Raj structure there should be a two tier set up, i.e., a district level, Zila Parishad and a mandal Panchayat covering a population of 15,000 to 20,000.
2. With the two-tier structure, the committee also suggested unit of development administration.
3. I have already stated that I am in full support of the idea of a two-tier Panchayati Raj the larger panchayat which has been given in the report the name a mandal panchayat and the Zila Parishad. I am in support of it because of the general consideration that the two-tier set up is likely to be less expensive and more effective as well as may own experience in Kerala.
4. I oppose the recommendation in favour of a qualified Judge to preside over an elected Nayaya Panchayat being associated with him. The report itself admits that there is no enthusiasm for Nayaya Panchayat, the reasons being that people do not expect elected panchayats to be objective and do justice to the poor. Any proposal for bringing the judiciary closer to the people, can, therefore, be considered only as a matter of reforming the judicial system and not as a part of democratic decentralization of administration, the government may consider the various reports, referred to in our report, separately and not as part of strengthening Panchayat Raj.
5. Political parties could participate in the Panchayati Raj elections.
6. Elections to Panchayati Raj bodies should be conducted by the chief electoral officers of the states in consultation with the election commission.
7. Nayaya Panchayat should be kept separate from the development Panchayats. A qualified judge

should preside over them and elected panches should act as members of benches of Nyaya Panchayats.

8. Panchayati Raj bodies should normally not be superseded, but if suppression became necessary election should be held within six months.
9. Representation of the Scheduled Castes (SCs) and Scheduled Tribes (STs) in all Panchayat bodies should be no the basis of their population.
10. There is complete transfer of land, revenue collections to Panchayati Raj institutions over a period of five years.
11. A permanent annual grant of not less than Rupees 2.50 per capita should be made to the mandal panchayats.
12. The committee agreed to the need for some provisions in the constitution in order to provide the Panchayati Raj institutions the requisite status as well as assurance of continuous functioning and wanted that this aspect should be considered.

The Phase of Revival (1983 onwards)

After 1983, Panchayati Raj Institutions entered in an era of progress and prosperity. The assumption of office of the Prime Minister by Rajiv Gandhi itself made basic, drastic and fundamental changes in the revival, restoration and revitalization of the basic ideals of the PRIs. After Rajiv Gandhi came to power, he made sincere and whole-hearted efforts to implement the Panchayati Raj in letter and spirit. The scheme of Panchayati Raj as unfolded by him was the most comprehensive and radical blueprint of participatory democracy. He showed the necessary stamina and political will to implement this plan. He not only altered the basic character of the district administration but also unleashed forces which would bring profound changes in the relationship between the state and central governments. After decades of neglect, democratic decentralization-Panchayati Raj has moved centre-stage again. Democracy without Panchayati Raj is a negation of Mahatma Gandhi's dreams. Development with out Panchayati Raj is a negation of Jawaharlal Nehru's vision "Real change" said Nehru "comes of course, from within the village, from the very people living in the village and is not imposed from outside".

In this context, an attempt has been made to highlight critically the revival phase of Panchayati Raj from G.V.K. Rao Committee (1985) to the steps takes by the central government headed by Shri Viswanath Pratap Singh to the conferment of constitutional status.

From 1985 to 1992 was the period of serious thinking at the national level in favour of giving constitutional status to Panchayati Raj Institutions. The initiative in this regard was taken by Rajiv Gandhi during his period as Prime Minister. In those years, there had been growing serious concern in the country in regard the unsound status of Panchayati Raj Institutions in most of the states. It had been widely recognized by the government, public leaders and intelligentsia that the Panchayati Raj Institutions have not been able to "acquire the status and dignity of viable and responsive people's bodies". The main reasons for this are absence of regular elections, prolonged suppressions, insufficient representation of weaker sections like Scheduled Castes, Scheduled Tribes and women, inadequate devolution of powers and lack of financial resources.

Though Article 40 of the Constitution of India has directed the Indian states to organise and empower village Panchayats to enable them to function as units of self-government, yet most of the state governments have actually tended to pay only half-hearted attention to this directive. The Union government felt the need to "enshrine in the constitution certain basic and essential features of the Panchayati Raj Institutions to impart certainty continuity and strength to them."

For this purpose, the bold initiative taken by late Prime Minister Rajiv Gandhi to grant constitutional status and backing to rural (Panchayats) and urban (nagarpalikas) local self-government institutions and thereby deepen and strengthen our democratic system and ensure the involvement and participation of people in the preparation and implementation of programmes and schemes of economic development and social justice, has come to fruition now the 73rd Constitution Amendment Act 1992 mandates a uniform P.R. System. Through Amended at 1992 mandates a uniform Panchayati Raj Institutions Systems throughout the country except of some specified tribal and hill regions and stat in which special arrangement exits.

The Panchayati Raj Bill 1989

It is in this background that the constitution (sixty fourth Amendment) Bill 1989 was introduced in the Lok Sabha on May 16, 1989. The salient features of bill are summarised below:

The amendment proposed to insert Article 243 in the Constitution of India. This is to be the sole provisions in a newly added part viz., Part IX the Panchayats.

Structure: The bill proposed for making it obligatory for all states to establish a three-tier system Panchayat at village intermediate and district levels – with the exception of states which have a population not exceeding 20 lakhs where states may not constitute Panchayat the intermediate level.

Popular Participation

The bill proposed to provide for all seats in Panchayats at all levels to be filled by direct election. But state legislatures may provide for the representation in Panchayats of members of the house of the people and of the legislatives assembly and chairpersons of Panchayats at the immediately lower level without voting rights. The chairpersons of a Panchayats will be elected by the elected members of that body form amongst themselves.

Reservation: To ensure that scheduled castes scheduled tribes and women get adequate representation seats have been reserved for them. To ensure adequate representation so women, as nearly as 30 per cent of the total number of seats to be filled by direct election in every Panchayat shall be reserved for women and it shall be allotted by rotation to different constituencies in a Panchayat. The number of seats reserved for the scheduled castes and scheduled tribes in every Panchayat will be in the same proportion as the population of SC or ST to the total population of that Panchayat area. Act any rate, at least one seat shall be reserved for women of the seats reserved for SC and ST, and 33 per cent would be reserved to women belonging to SC or ST. However, the state legislature may provide for the reservation of the office of chairpersons the scheduled tribes and women. Only the elected members have the right to vote in the meeting of the Panchayat.

The Constitution (Sixty-Fourth Amendment) Bill introduced in the Lok Sabha in July 1989 aroused nation-wide controversy. The major points of criticism charged against the bill were:

(a) The idea of Panchayati Raj was a sudden brain wave or child of the ruling Congress Party fully aimed at immediate electoral gains. At the time of the general elections of 1985 Panchayati Raj was not at all a promise of the election manifesto. It shows that the Congress lacks a genuine commitment to the plan of decentralisation.

(b) The proposed changes in the bill affect the basic federal fabric of the nation. Certainly it will also adversely affect the centre state relation too. It is also to be noted that the proposed concerned bill was introduced in May 1989, when only six months were left for the general elections.

(c) The centre's motivation to amend the constitution in a bid to strengthen the grass-roots government was suspected by many in the country.

Though the controversial bill was passed by the Lok Sabha but fell in the upper house, in which the congress did not command majority. Soon the congress found itself out of Power. But the successor of Rajiv Gandhi, V.P. Singh introduced the Amendment Bill in September 1990. But it could not be passed due to the collapse of his government. It was followed by General Elections in 1991. The new Congress government headed by Sri P.V. Narasimha Rao picked up the thread initiated by Rajiv Gandhi. But one noticeable feature was that unlike Rajiv Gandhi. Rao had consulted all major political parties in the drafting of the bill. This is known as the Seventy Third (73) Constitution Amendment Bill 1991. It was passed by parliament in May 1993, on its satisfaction by fifty percent of the states. It's important features can be summed up as follows:

I. Structure

(a) Firstly there will be a gram sabha in each village. It will be a body consisting of all persons registered as voters in the Panchayat area at the village level. The Gram Sabha may exercise such power and perform such functions entrusted to it by the state legislature.

(b) There shall be a three-tier system of Panchayati Raj-village intermediate and district level in all States except state having population of 20 lakhs, which shall have the option not to have intermediate level bodies.

(c) There shall be direct election to fill all the seats in all three-tiers and state have been empowered to have option of ex-officio persons, like-Chairperson of the Panchayat body. MLAs, MPs and MLCs as ex-officio members.

(d) Panchayats have been given option to have Sarpanch of the village Panchayats to be elected either directly or from amongst the elected members.

II. Reservation for SC/ST

The constitutional amendment bill clearly provided for reservation of seats for SC/ST in Panchayats on the population basis.

III. It is also provided for reservation for women in general. Thirdly, as per the new Act, one third of the seats are to be reserved for women. Reservation should be on rotation basis. Similarly not less than one-third of the offices of chairman are to be reserved for women. These too are to be on rotation basis.

IV. Duration of Panchayats :

Fourthly, the Act provides for a uniform five-year term for PRIs. Thus there is no provision of any extension of period of five years and election shall have to be made before the expiry of period. Elections should be conducted under the supervision of the state election commission appointed by the state governor.

V. Appointment of finance Commission: According to Article 343-1 a Finance Commission has to be constituted to review the financial position of the Panchayats and to make recommendations to the government. The recommendations should be submitted to the governor who shall place it before the state legislature.

VI. **State Election Commission:** As cited earlier, according to the act there shall be separate State

Election Commission to conduct elections to the PRIs. The commission will work without any fear or favour for Preparation of electoral rolls and conduct of elections.

Thus the Panchayati Raj Act, 1992 constitute a major milestone in the history of rural Local Government, as it made elections to the PRIs mandatory at every five years. It guarantees the right of Local Self-Government institutions to exist independent of the whims and political colour of the State government. Further the Amendment has made are PRIs financial solvent. Moreover, the statutory compulsory representations of the weaker sections are assured in the PRIs. Lastly yet another warning feature is that the PRIs have been made more broad based which will rescue them from possible domination by the socially and economically well-off sections. Consequent upon the passing the new Act, all most all state government have enacted their own Panchayat Raj legislations.

73rd Constitutional Amendment Act 1992

The 73rd Constitutional Amendment Act 1992 introduced Part IX in the constitution of India regarding the structure, composition, election and scope of powers of Panchayats at the district, intermediate and village levels. The XI Schedule added to the constitution lists the subjects under which powers and functions could be given to Panchayats at district/intermediate /village levels.

Until the 73rd amendment was passed formation, structure, composition, powers, functions elections and such other matters regarding Panchayats were entirely looked after by the state legislature and government. With the coming into effect of the 73rd Constitution Amendment Act, the legislative and executive action of the state legislatures and governments as regards Panchayats will have to be now in accordance with the provision of Part IX of the constitution. The salient features of the Act are summarised as follows:

There shall be a gram sabha comprising all the registered voters of that Panchayat circle in which Gram Panchayat exercising such powers and performing such functions at the village level as the legislature of a state may provide by low.

A three-tier system of Panchayati Raj has to be constituted from village to block and to district levels in a state but the state with the population of less than 20 lakhs may not have the intermediate tier if it likes. The provision for the composition of the Panchayat at each level is to be made statutory by the state legislature. Seats in the Panchayats at each level are to be filled by direct elections. The state legislature, however, may provide for ex-officio membership in the district level and intermediate level Panchayats for chairpersons of the Panchayats located at the level below.

Reservation of seats for SCs and STs has been provided in proportion to their population at each level. Not less than one-third of the total membership has been third of the total membership has been reserved for women and these may be allotted by rotation to different constituencies in a panchayat. Similarly, reservation has also been made in respect of office of the chairperson for women.

A uniform term of five years has been provided for the PRIs and in the events of suppressions, elections to constitute the body should be completed before the expiry of six months from the date of suppression.

The state legislature have been given the power to authorize Panchayats to levy, collect and appropriate suitable local taxes and also provide for making grants in-aid to panchayats from the consolidated fund of the concerned state.

Panchayats shall be constituted in every state at the village, intermediate and district levels, thus bringing about uniformity in the PR structure. However, the states having a population not exceeding 20 lakh have been given the option of not having any panchayat at the intermediate level.

A Finance commission has to be constituted once in every five years to review the financial position of the Panchayats and to make suitable recommendations to the state on the distribution of funds between the state and local bodies with a view to ensuring continuity it has been provided in the Act that all the Panchayats existing immediately before the Commencement of the Act will continue till the expiry of their duration unless dissolved by a resolution to that effect passed by the state legislature concerned.

The state legislatures should bring in necessary amendments to their Panchayats acts within a maximum period one year from the commencement of the 73rd Amendment Act so as to conform to the provisions contained in the constitutions.

The Bihar Situation: After the Amendment in 1993, a conformity act was passed in Bihar that repealed earlier acts. For Bihar this was the third generation of Panchayati Raj Institutions (PRIs), the early two being its pre-independence and Balwantrai Mehta versions. The Ashoka Mehta Committee recommendations during 1970s did not bring any change in Bihar. Previous elections for LSG were held in 1978 under the acts of 1947 and 1961. After the new enactment fresh delimitation was done. The figure was 12162 Village Panchayats, 725 Panchayat Samiti and 55 Zila Parishads before the bifurcation of Bihar in November 2000. With the creation of Jharkhand, the figure came down to 8471:529:38. The Bihar Act, 1993 was amended in1995. Meanwhile; it was challenged in Patna High Court (HC) that struck down provisions regarding reservation for Other Backward Castes (OBCs) in proportion to their population, establishment of Gram Katchahary with the procedure of trial and suits and reservation of chairpersons' solitary posts at various levels in June 1996[33].

Bihar government filed Special Leave Petition (SLP) in the Supreme Court (SC) against the judgement. Elections were not held on the pretext of matter being sub-judice. Even the Working Group on Decentralised Planning and PRIs for the Tenth Five Year Plan (2002-2007) had felt that the concerned state governments were not vigorously pursuing the cases for their early hearing[34]

A turnaround came, when the SC clarified that there was no stay on elections and Patna HC issued mandamus in July 2000 to hold elections[35].

The salient features of the Bihar scheme were: recognition of Gram Sabha as a body for deliberation, decision making, and direct democratic participation at the grass-root level; uniform three tier structure based on population distribution; abolition of nomination and co-option, and direct election to all seats at all levels; direct election of Mukhiyas of Gram Panchayats and indirect election of Panchayat Samiti Pramukhs and Zila Parishad Chairpersons; reservation for the SCs and STs in proportion to their population for membership at all levels; reservation of not less than one-third seats for Women; five-years fixed tenure; devolution of powers and responsibilities; and setting up of State finance and state election commission. Elections were held in May-June 2001 generating a new subaltern resurgence accompanied with a wave of enthusiasm among women, Scheduled Castes (SCs) and Scheduled Tribes (STs)[36].

The new scheme of 2005/6- The new JD (U)-BJP coalition government withdrew the SLP from the SC and brought some significant changes in the existing scheme. It brought a new legislation reserving 50% seats and chairpersons posts for women. It also made 20% reservation for the extremely backward castes. Elected judicial machinery at Gram Panchayat level was also inserted[37]. Writ petitions against new scheme were not entertained by the Supreme Court and the High Court. Elections were held in early 2006.

References

1. Harold J. Laski, A Grammar of Politics, S. Chand, Delhi,1979, p. 411
2. Frank Cunningham, Theories of Democracy : A Critical Introduction, Routledge, London, 2002, p.82
3. Robert Putnam, Making Democracy Work, Princeton, New J, Princeton University Press, 1993, p. 173
4. Jane Mansbridge, "Does participation make better citizens"? The Good Society, 5.2 (Spring 1995), pp. 1-7.
5. Richard C. Crook and James Manor, Democracy and Decentralization in South Asia and West Africa, Cambridge University Press, 1998, p.2
6. United Nations, Summer Conference on Local Government in Africa, Cambridge, 1961 quoted in S.S. Meenakshisundaram, 'Decentralization in Developing Countries, in S. N. Jha and P. C. Mathur (eds.) Decentralisation and Local Politics, Sage, New Delhi, 2003, p.58.
7. Hugh Whalen, Ideology, Democracy and the Foundations of Local Self-Government, Methuen, Toronto, 1970 p.312
8. Will Durant quoted in S. R. Nigam, Local Government, S. Chand & Company, New Delhi, 1982, p.216.
9. M. Venkatarangaiya and M. Pattabhiram, Local Government in India: Select Readings, Allied Publishers, Bombay, 1969, p.1-2
10. M. K. Gandhi, Hind Swaraj or Indian Home Rule, Revised New Edition, Eighth Reprint, Navjivan Publication House, Ahmedabad, 1990

11. Gandhi's Views reproduced in M. Venkatarangaiya and M. Pattabhiram, Local Government in India: Select Readings, Allied Publishers, Bombay, 1969, p.247-8

12 Act No. X of 1842, passed by the Honourable the President in Council of India in Council on the 14th October 1842 with the assent of the Right Honourable the Governor-General of India, reproduced in N. 9 as Reading 4, pp.84-86

13. Act No. XXVI of 1850, passed by the Honourable the President in Council of India in Council on the 21st June 1850 with the assent of the most noble the Governor-General of India, reproduced in N. 9 as Reading 5, pp.86-90.

14. Lord Mayo's Resolution on Provincial Finance, 1870, reproduced in N.9 as Reading 7, pp.96-104

15. Gazette of India Supplement, April to June 1982, pp. 741-53, May 20,1982, Extract from the Proceedings of the Government of India in the Home Department(Public), dated Shimla, the 18th May, 1982, reproduced in N.9 as Reading 8, pp. 105-18

16. Recommendations of the Royal Commission on Decentralisation (1909) reproduced in N.9 as Reading 11, p.158-166.

17. S. R. Nigam, Local Government, S. Chand & Company, New Delhi, 1982, p.172.

18. Anugraha Narain Sinha, Mere Sansmaran, 2nd reprint, Kusum Prakashan, Patna, 1960, pp.117-26

19. Swami Sahajanand Saraswati, Mera Jeevan Sangarsh, Sitaramashram, Bihta, Patna, 1952, pp. 327-33

20. Jaya Prakash Narayan quoted in the commentary to the Reading 19, N. 9, 248.

21. Ambedkar's speech in Constituent Assembly, Relevant Debates reproduced in N.9, p.249-50

22. H.V. Kamath's speech in Constituent Assembly, quoted in N.9, pp.250-1

23. T. Prakasham speech in the Constituent Assembly reproduced in N.9, p.251
24. Alladi Krishnaswami Ayyar speech in the Constituent Assembly, ibid, p.251-2
25. N.G. Ranga's speech in the Constituent Assembly, N. 9, p.252
26. M. Ananthasayanam Ayyangar's speech in the Constituent Assembly, N. 9, p. 252
27. Mahavir Tyagi in Constituent Assembly Debates quoted in N.9, p. 252-3
28. N. Madhava Rao quoted in N. 9, p. 253
29. Nehru quoted in N. 17, p.175
30. Chandradeo Prasad, Bhartiya Sthaniya Swashasan, Bharati Bhavan, Patna, 1980,p.21
31. M.R. Biju, Dynamics of New Panchayati Raj System: Reflections and Retrospections, Kanishka Publishers and Distributors, New Delhi, 1998, p.22
32. Committee on Plan Projects, Report of the Team of the Study of Community Projects and National Extension Service, Vol. I, New Delhi,1957, p.7
33. Extract of the High Court order was published in the Times of India (Patna) for five consecutive days from June 22-26, 1996, p.12, p.6, p.12, p.12, p.12 and p.12.
34. Report, Planning Commission, November 2001, p.9
35. Extract of High Court order was published in the Times of India (Patna) on June 5-6, 2000, p.12, p.5.
36. Saibal Gupta, Hindustan Times(Patna), July, 2001, p.6 and also Ashok Kumar Pankaj and Mahendra Prasad Singh, 'The Changing Socio-Political Profile of Local Political Elites in Bihar: A Study of the 1978 and 2001 Elections', Contributions to Indian Sociology, 39:3, September-December 2005.
37. See, Sections-13, 15(5), 38, 40(2), 65, 67(2), 91and 93(5) of Bihar Panchayati Raj Ordinance, 2006.

2

Structural Framework

This chapter deals with the structural framework of the new Panchayati Raj System in Bihar. It covers the provisions contained in the Constitution (73rd) Amendment Act and the enabling enactments made by the Legislature in Bihar in 1993 and 2006/2007. It also covers the judgments delivered by the Patna High Court and the Supreme Court in this regard. This chapter ends with the discussion on the existing position. This chapter has been structured in four parts.

The first part deals with the salient features of the structural framework. It includes the composition of the three-tier structure of the Panchayati Raj Institutions (PRIs); various offices; the powers and functions of various bodies and functionaries of the three-tier PRI; the State Election Commission (SEC); the State Finance Commission (SFC); the District Planning Committee (DPC); etc.

The second part presents a detail discussion as to the composition of PRIs, reservation provisions and rosters, constituency size and offices. It also presents a discussion on the powers and functions of the Gram Sabha, Executive of the Gram Panchayat, Mukhia, Up-Mukhia, Gram

Katchahary, Sarpanch, Up-Sarpanch, Panchayat Samiti, Pramukh, Up-Pramukh, Vice-Chairman, Chairman, SEC, SFC, DPC, etc. It also discusses the composition, powers and functions of various committees at the levels of Panchayat Samiti and Zila Parishad.

In the third part of the present chapter, the discussion is mainly focused on interrelationship between various organs of the PRI structure. Particular attention has been given to this aspect between the Gram Sabha and the Panchayat Executive; the Gram Panchayat and the Panchayat Samiti; and the Panchayat Samiti and the Zila Parishad. It also covers the relations between various constitutional and executive authorities; and Panchayat bodies. It includes the role of the Governor, the State Government, Divisional Commissioner and the District Magistrate in the functioning of the PRIs. It also seeks to look into the influence exerted by these functionaries on PRIs and impact thereof on the autonomy of the PRIs. And also it looks into the role and influence of the State Planning Committee in this context.

The fourth part of this chapter presents a concluding summary of the structural framework as it obtained presently.

I

A: Salient Features

As discussed in the previous chapter, the year 1993 proved momentous in the evolution of local self government in India when it did not remain at the mercy of the concerned State government being confined at Entry 5 of the State List under Seventh Schedule and as a Directive Principles of State Policy at Article 40 under Part IV. Entry 5 read as, "Local Government, that is to say, the constitution and powers of municipal corporations, improvement trusts, district boards, mining settlement authorities and other local authorities for the purpose of local self-government or village administration." Article 40 reads as, "The State shall take steps to organise village Panchayats and endow them with such powers and authority as may be necessary to enable them to function as units of self government."

After the 1993 turnaround in self governance in India, provisions about these bodies found place in the Constitution of India as Part IX for the Panchayats and Part IXA for the Municipalities. Two schedules were added to the Constitution Sch. XI and Sch. XII which enlist the subject areas of these bodies. Constitution 73rd Amendment Act 1992 came into force with effect from April 24, 1993. The statement of its objects proclaimed that it was brought to impart certainty, continuity and strength to Panchayats. The Minister concerned, while introducing the bill in Lok Sabha, had said that the Government was fulfilling Mahatma Gandhi's dream of Gram Swaraj.[1]

Gandhi had said, "My idea of Village Swaraj is that it is complete republic, independent of its neighbours for its vital wants— the government of the village will be conducted by the Panchayat of five persons annually elected by the adult villagers, male and female— this will have all the authority and the jurisdiction required.[2]

As prescribed in the Amendment Act of 1993, a conformity act—Bihar Panchayati Raj Act of 1993— was passed that repealed the Bihar Panchayat Raj Act of 1947 and the Bihar Panchayat Samiti and Zila Parishad Act of 1961. For Bihar this was the third generation of Panchayat Raj Institutions, the early two being its pre-independence and Balwantrai Mehta versions. The Ashoka Mehta Committee recommendations during the 1970s did not bring any change in Bihar. Previous elections for PRIs were held in 1978 under the act of 1947 and 1961. After the 1993 enactment a fresh delimitation of Panchayats was done. In the pre-November 2000 scenario of undivided Bihar, that is prior to the creation of Jharkhand, the figure was 12162 village Panchayats, 725 Panchayat Samitis and 55 Zila Parishads. With the bifurcation of the State and creation of Jharkhand, the figure came down to 8471 village Panchayats, 529 Panchayat Samitis, 38 Zila Parishads.

The Bihar Act of 1993 was amended in 1995 that removed various difficulties and empowered the District Magistrate and the State government taking some functions respectively of the State Election Commission and the Governor/ Legislature.

The Bihar Act 1993 was challenged in the Patna High Court, which in its judgement in June 1996 struck down its various provisions. These provisions included reservation of seats for Other Backward Classes (OBCs) in proportion to their population, establishment of Gram Katchahary with the procedure of trials and suits, and reservation of chairpersons' solitary posts at various levels.[3] The Court had directed that the list of backward classes should be revised to exclude certain categories like Yadavs, Koeris and Kurmis who are politically well represented. It had also restricted the overall reservation to 50%. It directed that there should be no reservation to the posts of Mukhiya of a Gram Panchayat, Pramukh of a Panchayat Samiti and Adhyaksha of a Zila Parishad on the ground that these are solitary posts and these reservations would amount to 100% reservation.

Bihar government filed Special Leave Petitions (SLP) No.972428 and 981925 of 1996 in the Supreme Court against the judgement. Both these Special Leave petitions were filed challenging the Orders dated 19 March 1996 of Patna High Court in CWJC No. 3351/1994 and a batch of similar petitions. Elections were not held on the pretext of matter being sub-judice.

However on constant prodding through Public Interest Litigations, a turnaround came in the year 2000. On 29th August 2000, a Constitution Bench of the Supreme Court clarified that there was no bar for holding elections to different Panchayats in accordance with law, as it stands today, which will be subject to the final decision in the pending appeals. The Court also directed the parties to urge before the Chief Justice of India for early hearing of the SLPs. The Patna High Court issued mandamus in July 2000 to hold elections.[4] In pursuance of the said Orders, The Government of Bihar issued orders that there shall be no reservation of any sort for the offices of Chairpersons in all the three tires of Panchayats, each of which being single post. The Bihar State Election Commission filed an Application seeking clarification whether Panchayat Elections could be held in Bihar in accordance with the law enshrined in Article 243D(4) of the Constitution of India reserving offices of Chairpersons in three tiers of Panchayats in favour of Scheduled Castes, Scheduled Tribes and women. This application came up for hearing on 5th January, 2001 in the Supreme Court. After the Advocate who appeared for Bihar State Election Commission, the Court dismissed it observing that as certain provisions of the Constitution had been struck down by the Patna High Court; such provisions could be treated as existing law until and unless those are restored by the Apex Court. Panchayat elections were held in April 2001 without providing reservation for SCs/STs/women to offices of Chairpersons of all the three tiers[5]. Even the Working Group on Decentralised Planning and PRIs for the Tenth Five Year Plan (2000-2007) had felt that the concerned state governments were not vigorously pursuing the cases for their early hearing.[6]

The salient features of the Bihar scheme were (i) recognition of Gram Sabha as a body for deliberation, decision-making and direct democratic participation at the grass-root level; (ii) uniform three tier structure based on population distribution—500 for a village Panchayat ward, 7000 for a Village Panchayat, 5000 for a ward (territorial constituency) of Panchayat Samiti and 50,000 for a ward (territorial constituency) of Zila Parishad; (iii) abolition of nomination and co-option and direct election to all seats at all the three levels; (iv) direct election of Mukhia of Gram Panchayat and indirect election of Up-Mukhia of Gram Panchayat, Pramukhs and Up-Pramukh of Panchayat Samiti; and Chairperson and Vice Chairperson of Zila Parishad; (v) reservation for the Scheduled Castes and Scheduled Tribes in proportion to their population for membership at all levels; (vi) reservation of not less than one-third seats for women; (vii) five years fixed tenure; (viii) devolution of powers and responsibilities; and (ix) setting up of the State Finance Commission (SFC) and the State Election Commission (SEC).

Elections were held in May-June 2001. It generated a new subaltern resurgence accompanied with a wave of enthusiasm among women, SCs and STs.[7]

In November 2005, a new JD (U) – BJP coalition government came to power in Bihar. It withdrew the SLP from the Supreme Court and proposed significant changes in the existing scheme. It brought a new legislation—Bihar Panchayat Raj Ordinance 2006—that came into force on January 18, 2006 replaced by an Act. The 2006 scheme has certain new features. It provided for reservation of fifty-percent seats of member and posts of chairpersons at all levels for women. It also provided for twenty percent reservation of seats of members and posts of Chairpersons for the Extremely Backward of Castes i.e. I Annexure / castes. It also provided for elected judicial machinery Gram Katchahary—at Village Panchayat level.[8]

Writ petitions against the new scheme were not entertained by the Supreme Court and the High Court. Elections were held in early 2006.

B. Structure and Functions

Gram Panchayat

So far as the composition of Gram Panchayat is

concerned, it comprises of the Mukhia, who is directly elected and a number of directly elected members representing nearly a population of 500. The District Magistrate has been empowered to divide the area of the Gram Panchayat into territorial constituencies under the direction, control and supervision of the State Election Commission in such a manner that the population of each territorial constituency be the same throughout the Gram Panchayat area. The District Magistrate follows the rules made by the State Government in this regard. One member is elected from each territorial constituency through direct election.[9]

Panchayat Samiti

The Panchayat Samiti is the second tier of the Panchayat Raj System. So far as its composition is concerned, it consists of –

(a) directly elected members from the Panchayat Samiti's territorial constituencies;

(b) members of the Lok Sabha and the members of the Bihar Legislative Assembly, representing constituencies which fall either wholly or partly in the Panchayat Samiti area;

(c) members of Rajya Sabha, and the members of the Bihar Legislative Council who are registered as electors within the Panchayat Samiti area; and

(d) all the Mukhiyas of the Gram Panchayats.

It has been made clear that every member of the Panchayat Samiti have the right to vote in its meeting. But in case of election and removal of Pramukh and Up-Pramukh, only the members elected directly from the people for the purpose from a territorial constituency comprised of the population of 5000 have the right to vote.

Like the division of the area of Gram Panchayat, the D.M. is also empowered to divide the Panchayat Samiti area in accordance with the rules and under the direction, control and supervision of the State Election Commission. From each territorial constituency one member is directly elected.[10]

Zila Parishad

The Zila Parishad is the third and the highest-tier of the Panchayat Raj System. The Zila Parishad consists the directly elected members from territorial constituencies in the district; the Pramukhs of all Panchayat Samitis in the District; such members of Lok Sabha and members of the Bihar Legislative Assembly representing any part that fall wholly or partly within the district and whose constituency fall within the district; and the members of the Rajya Sabha and the members of Bihar Legislative Council registered as electors within the district.

Every member of the Zila Parishad has the right to vote in its meeting. But in case of election and removal of Adhyaksha and Up-Adhyaksha only the directly-elected members have the right to vote.

The District Magistrate have been empowered to determine the number of directly elected members from the Zila Parishad's territorial constituencies, keeping in view the overall population of the district at a rate of one member, as nearly as possible, for every 50,000 population.

For the convenience of election, the District Magistrate follows the rules prescribed by the State Government for dividing the area of Zila Parishad. The District Magistrate acts under the direction, control and supervision of the State Election Commission while dividing the area into territorial constituencies. He acts in a manner that the population of each territorial constituency, as far as practicable, be the same throughout the Zila Parishad area. One member from each territorial constituency is to be elected through direct election.[11]

Gram Sabha

Gram Sabha is a body that consists of all the registered voters of a Gram Panchayat area. It is an unique body. It is an embodiment of direct democracy as well as participatory democracy in real terms. The 73rd Amendment Act provided it constitutional and legal status for the first time. The Gram Sabha exercises powers and performs functions at the village level as provided by the State in the Act. As regards the period of its meetings, the Bihar Act provides that the Gram Sabha would meet at least four times in a year.[12]

It specifies that not more than three months should intervene in between any of the two meetings of the Gram Sabha, the embodiment of grassroots democracy.

As regards convening of meetings of the Gram Sabha, a notice needs to be pasted in the office of the Gram Panchayat and the same has also be brought to the notice of the public by beat of drum or by any other means of publicity. The Act prescribes means for the prior publicity of its meetings. It also prescribes the procedure for convening and conducting of its meetings.

The Mukhia of Gram Panchayat has been made responsible for convening the meeting of the Gram Sabha at regular intervals. In case he fails to convene the meeting, the Executive officer of the Panchayat Samiti has to convene meeting on being informed of this omission. The Executive Officer has to depute a Government Servant to be present in such a meeting on his behalf.[13]

Meeting and Quorum

Regarding quorum for a meeting of the Gram Sabha, it has been prescribed that one-twentieth of the total members of the Gram Sabha constitute it. It has also been provided that, if at the time appointed for the meeting, a quorum is not complete or if the meeting has begun and attention is drawn towards lack of quorum, the presiding authority shall wait for one hour and if within such period there is no quorum, the presiding authority shall adjourn the meeting to such time on the following day or such further day as he may fix. The business which could not be considered at the meeting so postponed for want of quorum shall be brought before and disposed of at the subsequent adjourned meeting or meetings for which a quorum of one-fortieth of the total members of the Gram Sabha shall be required. So it is clear that the adjourned meeting can be held at reduced quorum requirement.[14]

So far as the presiding officer for the meeting of the Gram Sabha is concerned, the Mukhiya of the concerned Gram Panchayat was to preside it. In the absence of Mukhiya, Up-Mukhiya was to preside it.[15]

Vigilance Committee of the Gram Sabha

The Vigilance Committee is a unique institution. The Gram Sabha has to form one or more vigilance committee (s) consisting of persons who are not members of the Gram Panchayat, to supervise the Gram Panchayat works, schemes and other activities relating to that village and to put up reports related to them in its meeting.[16]

Reservation of the Seats

According to Bihar Panchayati Raj Act 1993, reservation of seats for Scheduled Castes (SCs), Scheduled Tribes (STs) and the Backward Classes (OBCs) were made in the Panchayat Raj Institutions—Gram Panchayat, Panchayat Samiti & Zila Parishad.

The Act prescribed that the number of seats so reserved should bear as nearly as may be practicable the same proportion to the total number of seats to be filled up by direct election on that Panchayat Raj Institution as the population of the SC/ST and Backward classes, bears to the total population of that area and such seats should be allotted by rotation to different constituencies in a Panchayat Raj Institution.

It will be decided by the District Magistrate under the direction, control, supervision of the State Election Commission in the manner prescribed.

Women's Reservation

It provides that no less than one-third of the total number of seats reserved for SCs, STs and OBCs shall be reserved for women belonging to the SCs/STs or the Backward classes as the case may be. It also provides that no less than one-third, including the number of seats reserved for women belonging to the SCs, STs, and Backward classes, of the total number of the seats to be filled through direct election in every PRIs, should be reserved for women. Such seats would be allotted by rotation, of the different constituencies.[17]

The Article 243D of the Constitution of India explicitly provided for the reservation of SCs and STs and women. The decision regarding reservation of seats in any Panchayat or offices of Chairpersons in the Panchayats at any level in favour of the backward class of citizens was left at the discretion of the State Legislature [243 D (6)]. Sections 13 (1), 36 (1) and 63 (1) of 1993 Act amended in 1995 provided for reservation of seats for OBCs in proportion to their population. These sections were declared *ultra vires* by the High Courts[18]. The court declared that since the scheme of combined reservation provided under sections 13 (1), 36 (1) and 63 (1) would exceed the permissible limits of 50% in view of the population strength of Scheduled castes, Scheduled Tribes and other Backward classes. It suffers from the vice of excessive reservation. The principle of proportionate representation with respect to backward classes should not be followed in view of the population strength of SC/ST which is between 20-24% and backward classes which is between 50-70%[19].

The new coalition government of the Janata (United)-Bhartiya Janata Party combine that came to power November 2005 after the elections for the Fourteenth Vidhan Sabha made some far-reaching changes in the scheme of reservation, particularly with respect to women and a section of the other backward classes. The job reservation scheme for OBCs prevalent in state government jobs have been distinguishing between the extremely backward castes (EBCs) mentioned in Annexure I and the relatively advanced other backward castes mentioned in Annexure II. The JD(U) - BJP government decided to provide reservation for the EBCs. Twenty percent seats and posts could be reserved for them. And for Women, altogether fifty percent seats at all levels were reserved. Reservation for SCs, STs, EBCs and women were also made to the solitary posts of Chairperson, Pramukh and Mukhia. However, the High Court in Krishna Kumar Mishra vs. State of Bihar case (1996) had declared that reservation of the solitary post amounts to cent-percent reservation, which was not permissible. The court had taken 50% reservation permissible limit. In 1996 the court had declared that no reservation could be made for the post of Mukhiya/Pramukh/Adhyaksha. Though, Constitution of India under Article 243 D (4) had provided for it. The new government made reservation for the solitary post of Chairpersons also and the election were held in 2006 without any legal interference.

Reservation Scheme 2006

In Panchayati Raj Institutions at all levels—Gram Panchayat, Panchayats Samiti and Zila Parishad—as nearly as but not exceeding fifty (50) percent of the total seats of members of PRIs were reserved of SC/STs and Backward classes.

The number of seats was reserved for SC/STs in the

same proportion to the total number of seats to be filled up by direct election in that Gram Panchayat as the population of the SC/STs bore to the total population of that area. Such seats were to be allotted by rotation to different constituencies in a Gram Panchayat, Panchayat Samiti and Zila Parishad under the direction, control and supervision of the State Election Commission.

After reservation of seats for the SC/STs, the number of seats to be reserved should be as nearly as possible but not exceeding twenty percent of the total seats and within the overall limit of fifty percent reservation for the SCs/STs and the Backward Classes and shall be allotted to the remaining constituencies.

As nearly as but not exceeding fifty percent of the total number of seats reserved for SCs, STs and OBCs was to be reserved for women belonging to the SCs/STs and the Backward Classes.

Fifty Percent Reservation for Women

As nearly as but not exceeding fifty percent of the total number of seats not reserved for SC/STs and Backward Classes was to be reserved for women.

Such total number of seats reserved for women belonging to the SCs/STs and the Backward Classes and Unreserved Category was to be allotted by rotation by the District Magistrate under the direction, control and supervision of the State Election Commission, to different constituencies in Gram Panchayat, Panchayat Samiti and Zila Parishad area.[20]

Post of the Chairpersons

Reservation for the post of the Chairpersons in the Panchayat Raj Institutions was provided by Bihar Panchayati Raj Ordinance 2006. There was no reservation for these posts earlier as relevant section of the Bihar Panchayati Raj

Act, 1993, 1995 were nullified by the High Court.

For the post of Chairpersons, as nearly as but not exceeding fifty percent of the total seats of Mukhiya within every Panchayat Samiti, for the post of Pramukh within every District and for the post of Adhyaksha within every state was reserved for SCs/STs and Backward Classes.

Within every Panchayati Raj Institutions seats are reserved for SCs/STs and Backward Classes. For the post of Chairpersons, the number of seats are to be as nearly as possible the same proportion to the total number of seats of chairperson within the said PRIs as the population of SCs/STs bears to the proportion of the total population of that area and such seats shall be allotted by rotation to different institutions, under the direction, control and supervision of the State Election Commission in the prescribed manner.

After reservation of seats of the Chairpersons for the SCs/STs the number of seats to be reserved for the Backward Classes are to be as nearly as possible but not exceeding twenty percent of the total seats and within the overall limit of fifty percent reservation for the SCs/STs and the Backward Classes. These posts are to be allotted to the remaining Gram Panchayat and Panchayat Samiti by the District Magistrate and Zila Parishad posts by the State Election Commission. Such seats are to be allotted by rotation to different Gram Panchayat within a Panchayat Samiti and Panchayat Samiti within a district and Zila Parishad within the State.

As nearly as but not exceeding fifty percent of the total number of seats so reserved are to be reserved for women belonging to SCs/STs and Backward Classes.

As nearly as but not exceeding fifty percent of the total number of unreserved general seats are to be reserved for women.

Such total number of seats reserved for women

belonging to the SCs/STs and the Backward Classes and unreserved category are to be allotted by rotation by the District Magistrate under the direction, control and supervision of the State Election Commission to different constituencies in a Gram Panchayat, Panchayat Samiti and Zila Parishad in manner prescribed.[21]

Functions

Gram Sabha: Functions

The functional jurisdiction of the Gram Sabha is very wide. Matters for its consideration include the annual statement of accounts of the Gram Panchayat, the report of administration of the preceding financial year and the last audit note and replies. The Gram Sabha also considers the budget of the Gram Panchayat for the next financial year, the report in respect of development programmes of the Gram Panchayat relating to the preceding year and development programmes proposed to be undertaken during the current year.

It also considers the reports of the Vigilance Committee of the Gram Panchayat. Resolution relating to matters entrusted to the Gram Sabha has to be passed by a majority of the members present and voting in the meeting of the Gram Sabha.[22]

Further, the Gram Sabha has to perform the following functions.

1. It has to render assistance in the implementation of development schemes pertaining to the village.
2. It has to identify beneficiaries for the implementation of developmental schemes pertaining to the village. However, in case the Gram Sabha fails to identify the beneficiaries within a reasonable time, the Gram Panchayat shall identify the beneficiaries.
3. The Gram Sabha has to procure voluntary labour

and contributions, in kind or in cash or both, for community welfare programmes.

4. The Gram Sabha has to provide all assistance in the programmes of mass education and family welfare within the village.

5. It has to work toward promotion of unity and harmony among all sections of society in the village.

6. Its functions include seeking clarification from the Mukhia, Up-Mukhia and members of the Gram Panchayat about any particular activity, Scheme, income and expenditure.

7. It has been empowered to discuss and recommend appropriate action with regard to reports of the Vigilance Committees. Further, the Act provides that the Legislature and the State Government may prescribe other matters also for its functional role.[23]

Functions of Gram Panchayat

The Gram Panchayat has been assigned all functions, which a local government is normally expected to perform. Besides, it is looked upon as an instrument for execution of the community development programme. The Panchayat is also the agent of the State government for performance of certain specified tasks allotted to it. The functions of a Panchayat are usually classified into two types—obligatory and discretionary. The obligatory functions are those which a Panchayat shall perform, while discretionary functions are those which it may perform or shall have to perform if the state government so directs.

The general functions of the Gram Panchayat are as follows :

(1) Preparation of annual plans for the development of the Panchayat area;

(2) Preparation of annual budget;

(3) Power to take up relief works during natural calamities;

(4) Removal of encroachments on public properties;

(5) Organising voluntary labour and contribution for community works;

(6) Maintenance of essential statistics of village(s).

In addition to general functions, Gram Panchayats have certain other important functions.

Functions relating to agriculture include agriculture extension also. These are promotion and development of agriculture and horticulture; development of waste lands; and development and maintenance of grazing lands and preventing their unauthorized alienation and use.

Functions relating to Animal husbandry, dairy and poultry include improvement of breed of cattle, poultry and other livestock; Promotion of dairy farming, poultry and piggery; and Gram Panchayats have to undertake work in relation to fisheries also.

Social and farm forestry, minor forest produce, fuel and fodder are also within the functional jurisdiction of Gram Panchayats. It has been specified in the ordinance that these institutions have to look after planting and preservation of trees on the sides of roads and other public lands under its control, fuel plantations and folder development; promotion of farm forestry; and development of social forestry. Promotion of rural and cottage industries, organisation of awareness camps, seminars and training programmes, agricultural and industrial exhibitions for the benefit of rural areas are its assigned functions under the heading.

Rural Housing covering distribution of house sites within its jurisdiction and maintenance of records relating to house sites and other private and public properties is within the functional areas of the Gram Panchayat.

Functions related to drinking water like construction, repair and maintenance of drinking water wells, tanks, ponds and hand pumps; prevention and control of water pollution; and maintenance of rural water supply schemes also assigned to Gram Panchayats.

Roads, Buildings, culverts, bridges, ferries, waterways and other means of communication are to be constructed and maintained by it. Rural Electrification, including distribution of electricity and providing for and maintenance of lighting public streets and other places and promotion and development of non-conventional energy sources are to be done by Gram Panchayats. It can set up, develop and maintain community non-conventional energy devices. It has also to propagate other energy efficient devices within its area. Implementation of poverty alleviation programme is one of the special tasks of Gram Panchayats. It is to promote public awareness and participate in property alleviation programmes for fuller employment and creation of productive assets within its area. Presently National Rural Employment Guarantee Scheme is being implemented through the Gram Panchayats in accordance with the Central Act—National Rural Employment Guarantee Act.

Selection of beneficiaries under various rural development, poverty alleviation, welfare and social welfare programmes of the union and state governments are to be made through Gram Sabhas. Gram Panchayats have to participate in effective implementation and monitoring to poverty alleviation programmes according to the Bihar Act 1993 and Bihar ordinance 2006 also.

Functions related to education, including primary and secondary school education are given to Gram Panchayats. Promotion of public awareness is the first task. It has to participate in primary and secondary education. The task is to ensure full enrolment and attendance in primary schools and their management is assigned to Gram Panchayat. Under adult and non-formal education, it is entrusted with the task of promotion of mass literacy.

Village libraries and reading rooms are to be established and maintained by Gram Panchayats.

Cultural and Sports Activities

Promotion of social, cultural and sports activities, management of village markets and fairs, including cattle fairs and festivals are functions of Gram Panchayats. Maintenance of general sanitation; cleaning of public roads, drains, tanks, wells and other public places; maintenance and regulation of burning and burial grounds; construction and maintenance of public latrines; disposal of unclaimed corpses and carcasses; management and control of washing and bathing ghats and up gradation of environment and prevention of its degradation are its tasks under the heading rural sanitation and environment.

Public health and family welfare functions include. Implementation of family welfare programmes and public health centres; prevention of and taking remedial measures against epidemics; regulation of sale of meat, fish and other perishable food articles; participation in programmes of human and animal vaccination; Licensing of eating and entertainment establishment, regulation of curing, tanning and dyeing of skins and hides; and regulations of offensive and dangerous trades.

Women and child development are another important function of the Gram Panchayat. It includes participation in the implementation of women and child welfare programme, promotion of education, health and nutrition programmes.

Its social welfare functions include welfare of the physically and mentally challenged persons. It has to participate in the implementation of the social welfare programmes. Particular mention of destitute is made in this respect. The Gram Panchayats have to monitor the old-age and widows' pension schemes run by the government for the weaker sections and in particular the scheduled castes and scheduled tribes.

It has to promote public awareness, participate in the implementation of specific programmes for the welfare of the weaker sections. The functions of Gram Panchayat as regards food security are manifold. Awareness about the distribution of essential commodities and monitoring the public distribution system are the tasks of Gram Panchayats. Maintenance of community assets belonging to the Gram Panchayat and other community assets come within the preview of Gram Panchayats functional areas. Further construction and maintenance of dharamshalas, hostels and similar institutions are also listed in the Act. Construction and maintenance of cattle sheds, pounds and cart stands, slaughter houses, public parks, play ground etc. are enumerated as the function of Panchayats.

Regulation of garbage bins in public places, and establishment and control of huts and sheds also figure. The Act states that other functions may be entrusted to Gram Panchayats.[24]

Functions of Panchayat Samiti

Panchayat Samiti is the middle rung of the three-tier structure of the Panchayati Raj Institution as envisaged in the Constitution 73rd Amendment Act. This organ was in existence earlier also under the provisions of 1961 Zila Parishad and Panchayat Samiti Act. Though then it did not comprise of directly elected members, Mukhiyas constituted it along with co-opted ex-officio members. Under 1993 Act, this body came into existence in2001 with new, enlarged functions.

Its functions are listed in Chapter IV at Section 47. The state government is empowered to prescribe the conditions under which Panchayat Samiti can discharge its functions.

Functions and Powers of Panchayat Samiti

Panchayat Samiti is the middle rung of the three-tier structure of the Panchayati Raj Institutions as envisaged in the Constitution 73rd Amendment Act. This organ was in existence earlier also under the provisions of 1961 Zila Parishad and Panchayat Samiti Act. Through then it did not comprise of directly elected members, Mukhiyas constituted it along with co-opted and ex-officio members. Under 1993 Act, this body came into existence in 2001 with new, enlarged functions.

Its functions are listed in chapter IV at Section 47. The state government is empowered to prescribe the conditions under which Panchayat Samiti can discharge its functions. Preparation of the Annual plans in respect of the schemes entrusted to it by virtue of the Act and those assigned to it by the Government or the Zila Parishad and submission thereof to the Zila Parishad within the prescribed time for integration with the District plan are the primary tasks of Panchayat Samiti. This task includes consideration and consolidation of the Annual plans of all Gram Panchayats in the Samiti and submission of the consolidated plan to the Zila Parishad. Further, preparation Samiti and submission of the consolidated plan to the Zila Parishad is the responsibility of Panchayat Samiti. It has also to perform functions and executive works entrusted to it by the Government or the Zila Parishad. It has to provide relief in natural calamities.

Functions related to agriculture; dairy, poultry, animal husbandry; land improvement and soil conservation, minor irrigation, roads, poverty alleviation, welfare, education, health, etc. are assigned to it. These are detailed here under:

1. Agriculture (including Agricultural Extension) -

   (i) Promotion and development of agriculture and horticulture.

   (ii) Maintenance of agricultural seed farms and

horticultural nurseries.

(iii) Storing and distribution of insecticides and pesticides.

(iv) Propagation of improved methods of cultivation.

(v) Promotion of cultivation and marketing of vegetable, fruits and flowers.

(vi) Training of farmers and extension activities.

2. Land improvement and soil conservation – Assisting the Government and Zila Parishad in the implementation of land improvement and soil conservation programmes of the Government.

3. Minor Irrigation, Water Management and Watershed Development -

(i) Assisting the Government and Zila Parishad in the construction and maintenance of minor irrigation works.

(ii) Implementation of community and individual irrigation works.

4. Poverty Alleviation Programmes - Planning and implementation of Poverty alleviation programmes and schemes.

5. Animal Husbandary, Dairy and Poultry -

(i) Maintenance of veterinary and animal husbandry services.

(ii) Improvement of breed of cattle, poultry and other livestock.

(iii) Promotion of dairy farming, poultry and piggery.

(iv) Prevention of epidemics and contagious diseases.

6. Fisheries – Promotion of Fisheries development.

7. Khadi, village and cottage industries –

(i) Promotion of rural cottage industries.

(ii) Organisation of conferences, seminars and training programmes, agricultural and industrial exhibitions.

8. Rural Housing – Implementation of housing schemes and distribution of house sites in villages.

9. Drinking Water -

(i) Establishment, repairs and maintenance of rural water supply schemes.

(ii) Prevention and control of water pollution.

(iii) Implementation of rural sanitation schemes.

10. Social and Farm Forestry, Minor Forest Produce, Fuel and Fodder –

(i) Planting and preservation of trees on the sides of roads and other public lands under its control.

(ii) Fuel plantation and fodder development.

(iii) Promotion of Farm Forestry.

11. Roads, Buildings, Bridges, Ferries, Water Ways and other means of communication -

(i) Construction and maintenance of public roads, drains, culverts and other means of communications; which are not under the control of any other local authority or the Government.

(ii) Maintenance of any building or other property vested in the Panchayat Samiti.

(iii) Maintenance of boats, ferries and waterways.

12. Education, including Primary and Secondary schools -

(i) Promotion of Primary and Secondary Education.

(ii) Construction, repair and maintenance of primary school buildings.

(iii) Promotion of social education through youth clubs and mahila mandals.

13. Technical Training and Vocational Education – Promotion of rural artisan and vocational training.

14. Adult and Non-formal education – Implementation of Adult literacy.

15. Cultural Activities – Promotion of Social and cultural activities.

16. Market and Fairs – Regulation of fairs and festivals.

17. Health and Family Welfare –

(i) Promotion of health and family welfare programme.

(ii) Promotion if immunization and vaccination programmes.

(iii) Health and sanitation of fairs and festivals.

18. Women and Child Development functions of the Panchayat Samiti include

(i) promotion of programme relating to development of women and children,

(ii) promotion of health and nutrition programmes in the schools, and

(iii) promotion of participation of voluntary organizations in women and child development programmes.

19. Social Welfare programmes including welfare of the handicapped and mentally retarded and destitute; and monitoring the old age and widow's pension and pension for the handicapped are another important function of the Panchayat Samiti.

20. Promotion of Welfare of the weaker sections and in particular of the Scheduled Castes and Scheduled Tribes and promoting such Castes and Classes from Social in Justice and exploitation are also included -

21. Maintenance of Community assets -

(i) Maintaining all Community assets vested in it or transferred by the Government or any local authority of organization and preservation and maintenance of other community assets are the tasks of Panchayat Samitis.

22. Rural Electrification – Promotion of rural electrification.

23. Public Distribution System Distribution of Essential Commodities.

24. Co-operation – Promotion of co-operative activities.

25. Libraries – Promotion of libraries.

Other functions may also be entrusted to a Panchayat Samiti by the Zila Parishad or the state government. The State Government can also extend to it the functions entrusted by the central government. The state government, however, retains the power to withdraw or modify the functions assigned to Panchayat Samiti under the Act.

General powers of the Panchayat Samiti include to do all acts necessary for or incidental to the carrying out of the functions entrusted or delegated to it. The Panchayat Samiti may by notification delegate to the Executive officer or any other officer.[25]

Functions and Powers of Zila Parishad

Zila Parishad stands at the apex of the three-tier Panchayat Raj structure. It has wide range of functions and powers. A look at the list of its functions shows that the functions of Panchayat Samiti and Zila Parishad are almost similar and overlapping.

The list is being reproduced below –

The Zila Parishad has to perform the following functions:-

(1) Agriculture

(i) Promotion of measures to increase agricultural production and to popularize the use of improved agricultural implements and the adoption of improved agricultural practices.

(ii) Opening and maintenance of agricultural seed farms and commercial farms.

(iii) Establishing and maintenance of godowns.

(iv) Conducting agricultural fairs and exhibitions.

(v) Management of agricultural and horticultural extension and training centres.

(v) Training of farmers.

(vi) Land Improvement and Soil Conservation.

(2) Irrigation-Ground Water resources and watershed development -

(i) Construction, renovation and maintenance of minor irrigation works and lift irrigation.

(ii) Providing for timely and equitable distribution and full use of water under irrigation schemes under the control of the Zila Parishad.

(iii) Development of ground water resources.

(iv) Installation of community pump sets.

(v) Watershed development programme.

(3) Horticulture –

(i) Rural parks and gardens

(ii) Cultivation of fruits and vegetables

(iii) Farms.

(4) Statistics –

(i) Publication of Statistical and other information

relating to activities of Panchayat Samiti and Zila Parishad.

(ii) Co-ordination and use of Statistics and other information required for the activities of the Panchayat Samiti and Zila Parishad.

(iii) Periodical supervision and evaluation of projects and programmes entrusted to the Panchayat Samiti and Zila Parishad.

(5) Rural Electrification.

(6) Distribution of Essential Commodities.

(7) Soil Conservation –

(i) Soil conservation measures.

(ii) Land reclamation and land development works.

(8) Marketing –

(i) Development and regulation of markets and marketing yards.

(ii) Grading and quality control of agricultural products.

(9) Social Forestry –

(i) Organise Campaign for tree planting.

(ii) Planting and maintenance of trees.

(10) Animal Husbandry & Dairy –

(i) Establishment of veterinary Hospitals,

(ii) Setting up of mobile diagnostic and clinic laboratories.

(i) Breeding farms for cows and pigs.

(ii) Poultry farms, duck farms and goat farms.

(iii) Common cold storage facility for dairy, poultry and marine products.

(iv) Fodder development programmes.

(v) Promotion of dairy farming, poultry and piggery.

(vi) Prevention of epidemics and contagions diseases.

(11) Minor Forest Produce, Fuel and Fodder -

(i) Promotion of Social and farm forestry, fuel plantation and fodder development.

(ii) Management of minor forest produce of the forests raised in community lands.

(i) Development of wasteland.

(12) Fisheries –

(i) Fish seed production and distribution.

(ii) Development of pisciculture in private and community tanks.

(iii) Development of inland fisheries.

(ii) Fish curing and drying.

(iii) Assistance to traditional fishing.

(iv) Organising fish marketing co-operatives.

(v) Welfare schemes for the upliftment and development of fishermen.

(13) Household and Small Scale Industries (Including food processing) -

(i) Identification of traditional skills in the locality and development household industries.

(ii) Assessment of raw material requirement so as to ensure its timely supply.

(iii) Design and production to suit the changing consumer demands.

(iv) Organisation of training programmes for craftsmen and artisans.

(v) Liaison to tap bank credit for this programme.

(vi) Popularizing and marketing of finished products.

(vii) Industrial Estates.

(viii) Organising Khadi, Handloom, Handicraft and village and cottage industries.

(14) Rural Roads & inland waterways -

(i) Construction and maintenance of roads other than National and State Highways and bridges and culverts coming under these roads other than National and state highways.

(ii) Construction and maintenance of office building of the Zila Parishad.

(iii) Identification of major link roads connecting markets, educational institutions, health centres and link roads, and also organizing voluntary surrender of lands for new roads and for widening of existing roads.

(15) Health and Hygiene –

(i) Establishment and maintenance of hospitals, Primary Health Centres and dispensaries except Medical College Hospital, T. B. Sanatoriums, Leprosy Hospitals and Mental Hospitals.

(ii) Implementation of immunization and vaccination programme.

(iii) Health education activities.

(iv) Maternity and child health activities.

(v) Family welfare activities.

(vi) Organising health camps with Panchayat Samiti and Gram Panchayat.

(vii) Measures against environment pollution.

(16) Rural Housing -

(i) Identification of houseless families ;

(ii) Implementation of house building programme in the district.

(iii) Popularising low cost housing.

(17) Education -

(i) Promotion of educational activities including the establishment and maintenance of primary and secondary schools.

(ii) Organisation of programmes for adult education and library facilities.

(iii) Extension work for propagation of science and technology to rural areas.

(iv) Survey and evaluation of educational activities.

(v) Establishment and maintenance of general hostels, ashrams, schools and orphanages.

(18) Social Welfare and Welfare of Weaker Section -

(i) Extension of educational facilities to the Scheduled Castes, Scheduled Tribes and Backward classes by giving scholarships, stipends, boarding grant and other grants for the purchase of books and other accessories.

(ii) Managing hostels for the benefit of Scheduled caste and Scheduled tribes.

(iii) Organising nursery schools, balwadis, night schools and libraries to eradicate illiteracy and impart general education.

(iv) Conduct of model welfare centres and craft centres to train scheduled castes and scheduled tribes in cottage and rural industries.

(v) Managing residential basic schools for scheduled castes and scheduled tribes.

(vi) Providing facilities for marketing of goods produced by members of the scheduled castes and the scheduled tribes.

(vii) Organising co-operative societies of scheduled castes and scheduled tribes.

(viii) Other welfare schemes for the upliftment and development of scheduled castes and scheduled tribes.

(19) Poverty Alleviation Programmes – Planning, supervision, monitoring and implementation of poverty alleviation programme.

(20) Social Reform Activities –

(i) Women's organization and welfare.

(ii) Children's organization and welfare.

(iii) Local Vagrancy relief.

(iv) Maintenance of Social Welfare institutions such as orphanages, rescue shelters, etc.

(v) Sanctioning and distribution of pension for widows, old and physically disabled destitutes and allowances for unemployed and couples of inter-caste marriages in which one party is a member of a scheduled caste or a scheduled tribes.

(vi) Control of fire outbreak.

(vii) Campaign against superstition, casteism, untouchability, alcoholism, expensive marriages and social functions, dowry and conspicuous consumption.

(viii) Encouraging community marriages and inter-caste marriages.

(ix) Vigilance against economic offences such a smuggling, tax-evasion, food adulteration.

(x) Assistance for developing lands assigned to landless labourers.

(xi) Resumption of land alienated by tribals.

(xii) Identify, free and rehabilitate bounded labour.

(xiii) Organise cultural and recreational activities.

(xiv) Encouragement of sports and games and construction of rural stadium.

(xv) Give new form and social content to traditional festivals.

(xvi) Promotion of thrift and saving through;

a. Promotion of saving habits.

b. Small savings campaign.

c. Fight against money lending practices and rural indebtedness.

(21) In addition, the Zila Parishad may

(a) manage or maintain any work of public utility or any institution vested in it or under its control and management.

(b) Acquire and maintain village hats and markets.

(c) Make grants to Panchayat Samiti or Gram Panchayat.

(d) Adopt measures for the relief of distress.

(e) Coordinate and integrate the development plans and schemes prepared by Panchayat Samitis in the district.

(f) Examine and sanction the budget estimates of Panchayat Samiti in the district.

(g) Undertake or execute any scheme extending to more than one block.

(h) Takeover the maintenance and control of any rural bridge, tank, ghat, well channel or drain, belonging to a private owner or any other authority on such term as may be agreed upon.

(22) Zila Parishad can act in all such matters, as enumerated in the Eleventh Schedule of the Constitution of India and which are not mentioned any where under this Act.

(23) The Zila Parishad may be vested by the State Government with such powers under any Act as the Government may deem fit.

(24) The Zila Parishad of two or more adjacent districts may jointly undertake and execute any development scheme on such terms and conditions as may be mutually agreed upon.

(25) Preparation of annual budget of the Zila Parishad.

General Power of Zila Parishad -

(i) Subject to the general on special orders of the Government, the Zila Parishad may -

(a) Incur expenditure or education or medical relief outside its jurisdiction.

(b) Provide for carrying out any work or measures likely to promote health, safety, education, comfort, convenience or social or economic or cultural wellbeing of the inhabitants of district.

(c) Contribute to Associations at all India, State or inter-State level concerned with the promotion of local self Government and to exhibition, seminars and conferences within the district related to the activities of Panchayat Samiti and Zila Parishad; and

(d) Render financial or other assistance to any person for carrying on in the district any activity which is related to any of the functions of the State.

2. The Zila Parishad shall have Powers to do all acts necessary for or incidental to the carrying out of the functions entrusted or delegated to it and, in particular, and without prejudice to the foregoing powers to exercise all powers specified under this Act.[26]

Assignment of functions:

(i) The Government may assign to a Zila Parishad, functions in relation to any matters to which the executive authority of the Government extends or in respect of functions which have been assigned to the State Government by the Central Government.

(ii) The Government may notification withdraw or modify the functions assigned under this section.[27]

District Planning Committee

The District Planning Committee with its representative character is an unique body created at the district level under the provisions of the Constitution (73rd Amendment Act) 1993. The Planning Commission, Ministeries of Rural Development and Panchayati Raj have linked sanction and release of funds to districts in relation to all centrally sponsored schemes to this body. In Bihar, these bodies could be made effective only in 2006 under the new Act. Though, provisions as to their constitution existed in the Bihar Act of 1993 also. But the insistence of the union government has led to its establishment and functioning. It has been clearly stated by the union government that the State plans can be considered only when it is the aggregate of the district plans drawn and passed by the District Planning Committees.

So, any study of the working of the new Panchayati Raj System in Bihar even at the block level necessitates the inclusion of discussion over this body.

The Bihar Act asks the Government to constitute in every district, a District Planning Committee to consolidate the plans prepared by the Panchayats and Municipalities in the district and to prepare a draft development plan for the district as a whole. The District Planning Committee consists of:

(a) Adhyaksha of the Zila Parishad;

(b) Mayor or President of the Municipality having

jurisdiction over the headquarters of the District;

(c) Such number of persons not less than four-fifth of the total number of members of the committee as may be specified by the Government; elected in the prescribed manner, from amongst the members of the Panchayats and Municipalities in the district, in proportion to the ratio between the population of the rural areas and of the urban areas in the district under the direction, control and supervision of the State Election Commission :

It has been provided that a nearly as practicable, fifty percent of such elected members should be women;

It has been provided further that is there is no elected member from the scheduled castes, scheduled tribes or backward classes categories, the Government may nominate such number of members from SC/ST or Backward classes categories as it deems fit from amongst the members of the Panchayats and Municipalities in the district.

(3) Members of the Lok Sabha who represent the whole or part of the district, the members of the Rajya Sabha who are registered as electors in the district, all the members of the State Legislative Assembly whose constituencies lie within the district, the members of the State Legislative Council who are registered as electors in the district and the District Magistrate and the Chairman of the District Co-operative Bank/Land Development Bank are permanent invitees of the committee.

(4) The Chief Executive Officer of Zila Parishad shall be the Secretary of the Committee.

(5) The Adhyaksha of the Zila Parishad shall be the Chairman of the District Planning Committee.

The functions of the district Planning Committee include consolidation of the plans prepared by the Panchayats and

Municipalities in the district and preparing a draft development plan for the district as a whole.

The Act envisages the every District Planning Committee should in preparing the draft development plan have regard to -

(i) the matter of common interest between the Zila Parishad Panchayat Samitis, Gram Panchayats, Nagar Panchayats, Municipal Councils and the Municipal Corporations in the district including Local Planning, sharing of water and other physical and natural resource, the integrated development of infra-structure and environmental conservation.

(ii) the extent and type of available resources whether financial or otherwise.

(b) Consult such institutions and organizations as the Government may by order specify.

(6) The Chairman of every District Planning Committee have to forward the development plan, as recommended by such committee to the Government.[28]

State Finance Commission

The Act envisages the Constitution of a Finance Commission for Panchayat on every five year to review the financial position of the Zila Parishads, Panchayat Samitis and Gram Panchayats and to make recommendations to the Government. This body is similar to the Finance Commission at the Union level. It would determine the principles which should govern –

(i) the distribution between the state and the Panchayat Raj Institutions of the net proceeds of the taxes, duties and fees leviable by the Government. It would also suggest allocation between the Zila Parishads, Panchayat Samiti and Gram Panchayats of their respective shares of such proceeds. Further, it would suggest about the determination of the taxes, duties and fees which may be assigned to or appropriated by the Zila Parishads, Panchayat Samitis and Gram Panchayats. It would also suggest about the Grants-in-aid to Zila Parishads, Panchayat Samitis and Gram Panchayats from the consolidated Fund of Bihar. It would suggest the measures needed to improve the financial position of the Zila Parishads, Panchayat Samitis and Gram Panchayats. The State government can also refer any other matter to the Finance Commission in the interest of sound finance of the Zila Parishads.

So far as the composition of the Finance Commission is concerned, it consists of a chairman and two other members.

The state government is empowered to prescribe the qualification and manner of appointment of the chairman and members of the Finance Commission. The Finance Commission is authorized to determine its own procedure.

The Chairman or a member of the Finance Commission may resign his office by writing under this hand and addressed to the Finance Secretary to the Government. The casual vacancy created by the resignation of the member or chairman due to resignation or for any other reason may be filled by fresh appointment and a member or chairman so appointed shall hold office.

So far as the powers of the State Finance Commission are concerned, it has following powers in the performance of its functions namely: -

(a) to call for any record from any office or authority;

(b) to summon any person to give evidence or to produce records, and

(c) Such other powers as may be prescribed.

The Act specifically states that the Government shall cause every recommendation made by the Finance

Commission together with an explanatory memorandum as to the action taken thereon to be laid before both the Houses of the state legislature.[29]

State Election Commission

Like the Election Commission of India, a State Election Commission for superintendence, direction and control of the preparation of electoral rolls for, and the conduct of all elections to the Panchayati bodies has been provided in Part IX of the Constitution. So, the Bihar Panchayati Raj scheme has a State Election Commission to be appointed by the Governor.

(2) The conditions of service and tenure of office of the State Election Commission has to be determined by the Governor. It has been provided that the State Election Commissioner shall not be removed from his office except in like manner and on the like grounds as a Judge of the High Court and the condition of service of the State Election Commissioners shall not be varied to his disadvantage after his appointment.

(3) The Government is obliged on being requested to make available to the State Election commission officers and staff as may be necessary for the discharge of the functions conferred on the State Election Commission under the ordinance.[30]

Notification of Panchayat Election

The Governor, on the recommendation of the State Election Commission, for constituting the Panchayats and the Gram Katchahary, has to fix date or dates through notification published in the State Gazette. It has been provided that no such notification shall be issued prior to six months before the date fixed for election.[31]

So far as the administrative machinery for the conduct of Panchayat Election is concerned,

(1) The State Government have to make available to the State Election Commission, the services of officers and staff in the required numbers.

(2) The State Election Commission for the conduct of Panchayat election has to designate or nominate the District Magistrate as the District Election officer (Panchayat) for each district. It has also to designate or nominate one or more Deputy District Election officer (Panchayat) for the assistance of District Election Officer (Panchayat). This Deputy D.E.O. would not be below the rank of a Deputy Collector.

It has been provided that the District Election officer (Panchayat) subject to direction, control and supervision of the State Election Commission, has co-ordinate and supervise all works relating to conduct of election in the area within his jurisdiction.

For the Panchayat election, the State Election Commission or on being authorized by it, District Election Officer (Panchayat) shall appoint Returning officer (Panchayat) who shall not be below the rank of block. Development officer/circle /Deputy Collector and also appoint one or more Assistant Returning Officer (Panchayat).

The District Election officer (Panchayat) for every polling station, has to appoint a presiding officer (Panchayat) and to assist the presiding officer (Panchayat) polling officers.

It has been provided that any person who is a government servant or a servant of Government Company or servant of government aided institutions may be appointed as presiding officer (Panchayat) and polling officer.

Providing further that a polling officer on being absent from the polling station, the presiding officer (Panchayat) may under above proviso, appoint any person who is present at the polling station other than the persons appointed by the candidate or on is behalf or has been doing other work for him as polling officer and shall accordingly inform the District Election officer (Panchayat).

Provided further also that the polling officer subject to the direction of the State Election Commission, on being authorized by the presiding officer (Panchayat) perform all or any of the functions of presiding officer (Panchayat) under this ordinance and the rules framed there under.

If the presiding officer (Panchayat) owing to illness or any other unavoidable reason is compelled to be absent from the polling station then his functions shall be performed by such polling officer who has been so authorized previously by Returning officer (Panchayat) to perform such functions during such absence.

It shall be the general, duty of the presiding officer (Panchayat) to maintain order at the polling station and see that the poll is properly going on.

It shall be the duty of a polling officer of a polling station to assist the presiding officer (Panchayat) of such polling station in discharge of his functions.[32]

C: Inter-relationship Patters

Gram Panchayat and Gram Sabha –

Gram Sabha is the legislative body of Gram Panchayat. All the functional policies of Gram Panchayat has to be decided through the Gram Sabha.

There are two views of relationship between Gram Sabha and Gram Panchayat. One view is that Gram Sabha is the parent body and Gram Panchayat is its executive committee. There is also a view that both these bodies should operate as two separate entities and should function independently of one another. Another view is that Gram Sabha cannot enlist the Local people's interest if it lacks power to control the Panchayat, which is the executive. Gram Panchayat ought to be brought within the control of Gram Sabha without of course, damaging its effectiveness. Here lies the importance of the Mukhia as the head of Gram Sabha. He has a crucial role to play in making Gram Sabha an effective body without fanning confrontation.

The functioning of the Gram Sabhas since the constitutional amendment revealed certain weaknesses. In the first place, the Gram Sabhas are not taken seriously by the Panchayats and by the people themselves. Gram Sabha are treated more as recommendatory, advisory and suggestive bodies. They are expected to carry out important functions like consideration of the accounts of Gram Panchayats, audit reports, implementation of development programmes, but they hardly carry out such functions.[33]

Gram Panchayat and Panchayat Samiti

Gram Panchayat is the smallest institution of PRIs. The works of Gram Panchayat receives direction from the Panchayat Samiti. Every Panchayats budget has to be approved by the Panchayat Samiti. The role of Panchayat Samitis is to mediate and forward demands of Gram Panchayats to Zila Parishad. All the Mukhiyas are the members of Panchayat Samiti.

Panchayat Samiti, exercise supervision and control over Panchayats within its jurisdiction and what is more important, it provides necessary technical and financial assistance to them. It scrutinizes budgets of the Panchayats of the area under its control and makes suggestions about them.

Panchayat Samiti and Zila Parishad

Panchayati Samiti and Zila Parishad are the correlated institutions of Panchayati Raj System. The works of Panchayat Samiti has been done under the direction, supervision and control of Zila Parishad. All the development plans of Panchayat Samitis in Blocks are to be approved by the district level officers and Zila Parishads. It is one of the primary responsibility of these officials to assist the Zila Parishads and the Panchayat Samitis and also Block Development Officers and other extension officers at the block level to provide technical points of view and to ensure that supplies and services, which are basic to success to the developments plans are made in time and an adequate scale. Development officers at district level have a special responsibility for bringing about coordinated action in different bodies. The Zila Parishad has an important role in the preparation of rural works programmes. This works has been done through co-operation and suggestion by Panchayat Samitis. So scholars suggested that there should be harmonious relation between Zila Parishads and Panchayat Samitis.[34]

Zila Parishad and District Magistrate

It is an undeniable fact that the District Magistrates are playing a well defined role in the evolution of the Panchayati Raj System. The role of District Magistrates is as like a captain of a team of officers. All the development works has been done the directions of D. M. He has responsibility of securing necessary co-ordination in preparation and executive of district plans for the Zila Parishad.

It is a fact that all the functions of the Panchayati Raj Institutions are implemented under the direction, control and supervision of state government. District Magistrate has always functioned as an agent of the state government in a district. Effectiveness of the Panchayati Raj Institutions depends in no small measure on the co-operation of the district level officers as well as other organizations like municipalities and central and state government establishments in the district. This can be secured only by the District Magistrate.

District Magistrates are ears and eyes for the state government must remain fully informed of the cross currents of public opinion in his district. The source of this knowledge would get dried up if he is kept out of the Panchayati Raj System.[35]

Role of DDC –

The Deputy Development Commissioner is the Chief Executive Officer of the Zila Parishad. His role is crucial.

State Government and Panchayati Raj

The Panchayati Raj Institutions are subjected to wide ranging system of direction, control and regulation by the State government. Its control over the Panchayat Raj Institutions extends to almost every aspect. All its officers and staff are appointed by the state government or by the Governor of State. The secretaries have to keep and maintain all records of the Gram Panchayats. Other government officials have role in finance, administration of elections also. If a Panchayat fails to carry out a task, which it is obliged to undertake, the state government can get it done by an official appointed for this purpose and realise the expenditure from the Panchayat if it considers that the implementation of the resolution may spell danger to public life, health or property. If may suspend or remove a Panchayat Raj Institutions or a Sarpanch under certain conditions. It can even supersede a Panchayat, if the latter is consistently negligent of its duties. The device of grant-in-aid to the Panchayati Raj Institutions also enables the State government to exercise control over its activities.[36]

Conclusion

In this chapter, an attempt has been made to make an appraisal of the structural framework of Panchayat Raj Institutions (PRIs) in Bihar covering the Constitution Seven-third Amendment Act 1993, Bihar Panchayat Raj Act 1993 as amended up to 1995-1996, the relevant extracts of judgements delivered by the Patna High Court and the Supreme of India with regard of PRIs in Bihar and the provisions contained in the existing Bihar Panchayat Raj Ordinance (Act) 2006.

This chapter is structured into three parts besides a brief introduction in the beginning. The first part of this chapter dealt with the key features of the new Panchayat Raj System in Bihar. These features are three-tier organic structure, provision of reservation of seats and posts for the scheduled castes, scheduled tribes, Extremely Backward castes and women. It discusses the role of Gram Sabha as a body of direct-participatory democracy and also the rationale, functions and role of the State Election Commission and State Finance Commission.

In the second part, structure and functions of various bodies have been exhaustively presented. Various offices and their powers and functions have been analysed. In Bihar, the provisions as regard reservation of seats and posts carry certain features that are unique in certain respects. Particular mention may be made of fifty-percent reservation for women. In the second part of the present chapter, reservation roster, size of constituency etc. have also been discussed.

The third part focuses on the interrelationship between the three tier of PRI and also their relationship with the Divisional Commissioner, the District Magistrate, the Deputy Development Commissioner, the State Planning Committee, the State Government and the Governor.

The approach in this chapter has remained empirical depending on the primary sources.

In the next chapter devolution of functions, finance and functionaries to Panchayati Raj bodies on the basis of empirical data collection would be examined.

References

1. See Mahipal, 'Panchayati Raj and Rural Governance: Experience of a Decade', Economic and Political Weekly (2004) 39: 2, 138.

2. Reproduced in M. Venkatarangaiya and M. Pattabhiram, Local Government of India : Selected Readings, Allied Publishers, Calcutta, 1969, pp. 245-246.

3. Patna High Court in CWJC No. 3351 of 1994 and analogous cases disposed of a batch of writ petitions. Extract of the order was published in the Patna edited of the Times of India for five consecutive days from June 22 to 26, 1996 at p. 12, p. 6, p. 12, p. 12 and p. 12 respectively.

4. Extract of High Court order was published in the Patna edition of the Times of India on June 5-6, 2000, p. 12, p. 5.

5. 37th report of the Parliamentary Standing Committee on Urban and Rural Development, 2002, 101

6. Report, Working Group on Decentralised Planning and PRIs, Planning Commission, November, 2001, p. 9.

7. Ashok Kumar Pankaj and Mahendra Prasad Singh, 'The Changing Socio-political Profile of Local Political Elites in Bihar : A Study of the 1978 and 2001 Elections', Contributions to Indian Sociology 39 : 3, September-December 2005.

8. Selection 13, 15 (5), 38, 40 (2), 65, 67)2, 91 and 93 %) of Bihar Panchayati Raj Ordinance, 2006.

9. Chapter III Sec. 12, Bihar Panchayat Raj Act 1993 and also Bihar Panchayat Raj ordinance 2006, Chap. III Sec-12.

10. Chap. IV, Sec. 34, Act 1993, and also Chap. IV, Sec. 36, Act 2006.

11. Chap. V, Section 63 and 64, Act 2006 and also Chap. V, Sections 61 and 62, Act 1993.

12. Part IX Article 243-A, the Constitution 73rd Amendment Act 1992.

13. Chap. II,Sec-4 ordi. 2006 and also Sec.-4 Act 1993.
14. Chapter II, Section 5, Bihar Panchayat Raj Ordinance, 2006.
15. Chapter II, Section 6, Bihar Panchayat Raj Ordinance, 2006 and also Chapter II, Section 6 of the Bihar Act 1993.
16. Chap. II, Sec. 10 Act 1993 and also Chapter II Sec. 10 Ordinance 2006.
17. Chap. III Art 13, Chap IV Art. 36 and Chap V Art 63 B.P.R. Act 1993.
18. Krishna Kumar Mishra Vs. State of Bihar 1996 (1), PLJR 581
19. 1996 (1), PLJR 581
20. Chap. III Art. 13, Chap. IV/ Art 38 and Chap V /Art 65 Bihar Panchayat Raj Ordinance 2006.
21. Chap. III Art. 15 Sub Sec (5), Chap IV Art 40 Sub Sec (2) Chap. V Art 67 Sub Sec. (2) of Bihar Ordinance 2006.
22. Chap II Sec. 8 Ordinance 2006 and also Sec 8 Act 1993.
23. Chap II Sec 9 Act 1993 and also Chap II Sec. 9 ordinance 2006.
24. (Chap. III Sec. 22 Act 2006)

    Chap. III Sec. 22, Page No. 14 to 16, Act 1993.

    &

    Bihar Panchayat Raj Ordinance – 2006, Bihar Ordinance No.-1 of 2006, Law Publishing House Patna, Page No. 13 to 16.
25. Chap. IV Sec. 47 Act 2006, Chap. IV Sec-45 Act 1993 Page 31 to 33) Bihar Panchayat Raj Act, 1993 Malhotra Brothers.
26. Chap. IV Sec.-71, Act 1993 Page 45 to 49.

    Chap. V Sec-73 Ordinance 2006.
27. Chap-IV, Sec-73, Act 1993, Page No.-50.

    Chap. V, Sec-75 Ordinance 2006.

28. Chap. VI Sec- 167 Page,-95-96 ordinance 2006

Chap. VIII Sec. 134 Act 1993.

29. Chap. VII Section-168 ordi-2006.

30. Chap. VII Sec. 123 Page No. 72 ordinance 2006.

31. Chap. VII Sec-124, Page –72, Ordi. 2006.

32. Chap. VII Sec. – 125, Page 72, 73 ordi-2006.

33. S. R. Maheshwari, Local Government of India, Published by Lakshmi Narain Agarwal. Agra, Edition Tenth 2004, p. 82.

34. S. R. Maheshwari, Local Government in India, Page 116.

35. S. R. Maheshwari, Local Government of India, PP. 117-118.

36. S. R. Maheshwari, Local Govt. in India, P. 91.

3

Devolution of Functions, Finance and Functionaries

The 73rd Amendment to the Constitution of India envisaged a total change in the process of decentralized governance, planning, and development. The main objective of the Amendment was to delegate the task of preparation and implementation of plans for economic development and social justice to Panchayat Raj Institutions (PRI). The objective was sought to be achieved by giving constitutional status to elected Panchayats with a broad profile of the functions assigned to them in the selected sectors of development.

Article 243G says, subject to the provisions of this constitution, the Legislature of a state may, by law, endow the Panchayats with such powers and authority as may be necessary to enable them to function as institutions of self-government and such law may contain provisions for the devolution of powers and responsibilities upon Panchayats at the appropriate level, subject to such conditions as may be specified therein, with respect to –

(a) the preparation of plans for economic development and social justice;

(b) the implementation of schemes for economic development and social justice as may be entrusted to them including those in relation to the matters listed in the eleventh schedule.

The provisions contained in 243G and the XIth schedule are wide enough. However, the clauses underlined above, 'may, by law, endow'; and 'subject to such conditions as may be specified therein'. The States were required to devolve adequate powers and responsibilities on PRIs. The states were expected to place the functions of the Departments dealing with the 29 subjects listed in the 11th Schedule including the officials, under the control of the Panchayats. The functional autonomy of PRIs along with their financial autonomy was needed to be clear delineated. Even in respect of the 29subjects, it was necessary for the state governments to clearly identify what would be done by the different tiers of panchayats at each level.

Action on transfer of functions, functionaries and funds remained the key issue for the last 15 years since the constitution was amended, though at the local level self-government has been made ineluctable, irreversible and irremovable. Transfer of functions was to be based on the principle of subsidiarity. It means that any task that can be done by a lower level should not move to a higher level. It needs to be remembered that the processes and content of the devolution of functions, finances and functionaries are the crux of power to the Panchayats, which are vested entirely in state legislatures.

The key areas in which the general public need efficient and rightful access to public goods and services are precisely the 29 areas set out for devolution of powers. Devolution has three interrelated aspects of functions, finances and functionaries. These cover primary and secondary education, dispensaries and primary health care centres; drinking water; sanitation, rural housing; women and child development;

public distribution system, rural infrastructure, including roads, bridges and culverts and other elements of rural connectivity; veterinary centres; maintenance of community assets; rural industrialization, and everything related with minor irrigation and agriculture including agriculture extension.

The issue of devolution received utmost attention. Common minimum programme of the ruling United Progressive Alliance said :

The UPA Government with ensure that all funds given to states for implementation of poverty alleviation and rural development schemes by Panchayats are neither delayed nor diverted. Monitoring will be strict. In addition, after consultation with states, the UPA Government will consider crediting elected Panchayats with such funds directly.

Devolution of funds will be accompanied by similar devolution of functions and functionaries as well.[1]

In Bihar, elections for Panchayat Raj Institutions—Gram Panchayat, Panchayat Samiti and Zila Parishad—were held in 2001 and 2006. Several powers have been given to PRIs by the state government through devolution. Eighteen departments of the Government of Bihar had assigned specific powers and functions to these bodies in September 2001 itself:

A list containing such circulars is presented here:

1. Department of Agriculture – Memo No. 4/F / M-12/ 2001/3301 (Secy.) Ag; Patna 25.9.2001.
2. Department of Revenue and Land Reforms Memo No. 8/LR –Panchayt-22/2001-632R, Patna dated 26.9.2001.
3. Department of Water Resources (Minor Irrigation) Resolution..
4. Department of Animal Husbandry and Fisheries,

Resolution NO. 5M (1) 304/2001/AH/5647 dated 25 September 2001.

5. Department of Environment and Forest, NO. 10/2001-3087 dated 25 September 2001.
6. Industries Department, No. 3529 dated 24.9.2001.
7. Public Health Engineering Department, No. 6/1-2001-1169 dated 24.9.2001.
8. Rural Development Department, Resolution.
9. Rural Development Department for works of Panchayati Raj, Legislators and Kosi Kranti Schemes, CE-4/Misc-44/2001/707 dated 26.9.2001.
10. Department of Energy, No. 3073 dated 25.9.2001.
11. Department of Primary and Adult Education, 8/AR 3-431/1662, AE, 24.9.2001.
12. Department of Secondary Primary and Adult Education, 11/1-54/2001/986/Ed. Dated 25.9.2001.
13. Department of Art, Culture and Youth Affairs, No. 19/B2-11/2000/069 dated 25.9.2001.
14. Department of Health, Medical Education and Family Welfare, Memo No. 45 (18), dated 26.9.2001.
15. Department of Welfare, Memo No. 1/SC Misc. – 101/ 2001/3721 dated 24.9.2001.

15A. Department of Welfare Memo no. 5/SC A – 46/ 2001/3722 dated 24.9.2001.

16. Department of Social Welfare Letter No. 9/1CDS-12/ 2001/SW/32 dated 25.9.2001.
17. Department of Labour, Employment and Training (Directorate of Social Security) Memo no. 1/ P-1-107/ 2001 – LE / 1229 dated 24.9.2001 regarding maintenance of Statistics about migrant labourer, unemployed labourer, and employed/underemployed labourers.

17A. Department of Labour, Employment and Training (Directorate of Social Security) No. 1/P-1-2001-L.E./ 1230, dated 24.9.2001 regarding rehabilitation schemes for bonded labourers.

17B. Department of Labour, Employment and Training (Directorate of Social Security) letter no. 1231 dated 24.9.2001 regarding implementation of national maternity benefit scheme.

17C. Department of Labour, Employment and Training (Directorate of Social Security) No. 1/P1-107/2001/ LE/1232 dated 24.9.2001 regarding family benefit scheme.

17D. Department of Labour, Employment and Training, Memo No. MW-1029/2575 dated 24.9.2001 regarding monitoring and supervision of enforcement mechanism for Minimum Wages Act 1948 by the PRIs.

17E. Department of Labour, Employment and Training (Directorate of Social Security) No. 629 dated 25.9.2001 regarding social security pension scheme under State Plan.

18. Department of Food, Supply and Commerce, Memo No. Misc.-77/2001/4124 dated 26.9.2001 regarding devolution of powers and functions to PRIs.

19. Department of Relief and Rehabilitation, No. 1/N.C. 2-3/2001/1767 dated 25.9.2001 regarding devolution of powers.

19A. Department of Relief and Rehabilitation, No. 1435 dated 20.8.2001 regarding constitution of food/ drought relief monitoring committee at district and block levels.

37th Report of the Parliamentary Standing Committee on Urban and Rural Development was presented to the Lok Sabha speaker on 26.8.2002. The committee had examined the implementation of Part IX of the Constitution that is related to PRIs.[2]

On the status of devolution, the Committee noted that as transfer of regards funds, functions and functionaries connected with an the 29 subjects,/ departments were yet to be effected in Bihar.[3]

To accelerate the process of devolution and also demarcation of inter tier allocation of functions, the union government called a Conference of Panchayati Raj Ministers of States on 11th July 2001. The conference resolved that a Task force would be set up to suggest measured towards the administrative decentralization of funds, functions and functionaries upon Panchayats. A Task Force was constituted under the Chairmanship of Additional Secretary and Financial Advisor in the Ministry of Rural Development. The Task Force consisted of the State Secretaries in-charge of Panchayati Raj in Assam, Chattisgarh, Kerala, Karnataka, Pradesh and West Bengal with Joint Secretary dealing with Panchayati Raj in the Ministry of Rural Development as Member Secretary.

The Ministry of Rural Development forwarded a copy of the Report of State Governments and advised them to complete devolution powers upon Panchayats by 31st March 2002.

The Task Force examined the issue of devolution upon PRIs in detail. It suggested that it has to be carried out in terms of (a) transfers of functions, functionaries, funds; and financial autonomy. The Task Force submitted that all the 29 subjects/ Departments were yet to the transferred to Panchayats in Bihar.[4] Regarding status of District Planning Committee, it reported that it was not constituted.[5]

The Task Force report in Chapter VII presented activitywise devolution of powers upon PRIs with reference to functions, staff and organizational support alongwith

Funds as a guideline. Activity Mapping as recommended by the Task Force was commended by the Parliamentary Standing Committee appended it in its report.[6] The Task Force suggested that each State Government would have to prepare a framework in conformity with Article 243G and Eleventh Schedule to devolve appropriate powers to all the three tiers. The devolution of functions inevitably requires appropriate restructuring / reorganizing of the administrative set up at all the three levels.

The Task Force recommended that while the independent character of each independent character of each tier is to be maintained, there should be coordination among staff of different departments horizontally as well as vertically. Secondly The Chief Executive Officer of the Zila Parishad should be an officer equivalent to the District Collector in seniority and status for horizontal coordination.

Thirdly, till the integration of line departments with PRIs takes places, as a short-run measure the concerned District level Departmental Heads may be made accountable to the CEO of Zila Parishad. Fourthly, till a separate cadre of Staff meant for PRIs exclusively is created, the existing staff should initially be placed under the control of PRIs on deputation basis. Fifthly, all class I posts can be filled on deputation basis and class II officers should be either directly recruited through State Public Commission or brought on deputation, while Class III and lower staff should be recruited at regional or district level through an independent recruitment board.

The Parliamentary Standing Committee noted in 2002 that very few states seem to be serious about the implementation of the provisions of Part IX. The Committee said that endowing Panchayats with certain functions can be fruitful only if the PRIs are equipped with trained functionaries. It noted that Panchayats can fulfil their responsibility only if devolution is patterned on a nexus between the three Fs i.e. functions, functionaries and finances.

The Committee unhappily noted that barring Karnataka, Kerala and West Bengal, states have not linked the very important devolution of functions to the means of actualizing such devolution through the devolution of functionaries and finances. The pathetic lack of clarity about the tasks to be entrusted to different tiers of PRIs was lamented by the committee. It hoped that the activity mapping prepared by the Task Force would be a model for the State Governments, and they would sincerely make efforts to ensure devolution in the true spirit of the Constitution. The Committee also hoped that the State Governments would act in accordance with the pattern of capacity building of Panchayats that would result in their empowerment.

The Committee had recommended that Union Ministry of Rural Development be reconstituted as Ministry of Panchayats and Rural Development as the overall responsibility of monitoring the implementation of Part IX lies with the union government. This suggestion was implementation by the UPA government when on May 27, 2004 it constituted Ministry of Panchayat Raj with Mani Shankar Aiyyar as the cabinet minister. This ministry is engaged with monitoring the implementation of the 73rd Amendment and looks after capacity building and incentives for PRIs. As regards devolution of financial powers to Panchayats, the Constitutional provision in Article 243H as reproduced below specifies the powers to impose taxes by and funds to the Panchayats.

"The Legislative of a State may, by law, -

(a) authorize a Panchayat to levy, collect and appropriate such taxes, duties, tolls and fees in accordance with such procedure and subject to such limits;

(b) assign to a Panchayat such taxes, duties, tolls and fees levied and collected by the state government for such purposes and limits;

(c) provide for making such grants – in-aid to the Panchayats from the Consolidated Fund of the State; and

(d) provide for constitution of such funds for crediting all money received, respectively, and also for the withdrawal of such moneys there from, as many be specified in the law."

The statute with regard to powers of Panchayats under Article 243 H to impose taxes and raise revenue in Bihar is being presented below. Section 27 of Bihar Panchayati Raj Act, 2006 deals with taxation by Gram Panchayat. It says –

1. Subject to such rules as may be made in this behalf and the maximum rates specified by the Governments,

Gram Panchayat may impose yearly –

(a) Tax on occupation of holding;

(b) On professions, trades, callings and employments carried or held within the local limits of its jurisdiction a tax on the basis of total annual income accrued from such profession, trades, callings and employments.

2. Subject to such maximum rates as the Government may prescribe a Gram Panchayat may realize the following fees and rates, namely –

(a) Fees on registration of vehicles which are not registered under any other law in force at that time;

(b) Fees for providing sanitary arrangements at such places of pilgrimage, haats, melas and public use within its jurisdiction as may be specified by the Government by notification.

(c) Water Rate, where arrangement for the supply of water for drinking, irrigation or any other purpose made by or on behalf of the Gram Panchayat within its jurisdiction;

(d) Lighting Fee, where arrangement for lighting of public streets and places is made by or on behalf of the Gram Panchayat within its jurisdiction;

(e) Conservancy Rate, where arrangements for cleaning private latrines, urinals and cesspools in made by or on behalf of the Gram Panchayat within its jurisdiction.

Section 28 of Bihar Act deals with financial assistance to Gram Panchayats. It says : subject to the provisions of this section, every Gram Panchayat shall, after an appropriation made by law in this behalf, be entitled to receive grants in aid from the consolidated fund of the state as recommended by the State Finance Commission constituted under the provisions of this Act and as approved and notified by the State Government.

Section 55 of the Act deals with taxation by the Panchayat Samiti. It reads as:

(1) Subject to such rules and maximum rates as the Government may prescribe, a Panchayat Samiti may -

(a) levy tolls in respect of any ferry established by it or under its management;

(b) levy the following fees and rates, namely-

(i) fees on the registration of vehicles, which are not registered under any other law for the time being in force;

(ii) a fee for providing sanitary arrangements at such places of pilgrimage, haats, and melas within its jurisdiction as may be specified by the Government by notification.

(iii) A fee for licence for a haat or market,

(iv) A water rate, where arrangement for the supply of water for drinking, irrigation or any other purpose is made by or on behalf of the Panchayat Samiti within its jurisdiction.

(v) A lighting rate, where arrangement for lighting of public streets and places in made by or on behalf of the Panchayati Samiti within its jurisdiction.

To avoid overlapping, Sub-section (2) of Section 55 says that the Panchayat Samiti shall not undertake registration of vehicle or levy fee there for at places of pilgrimage, haats and melas within its jurisdiction or levy fee there for, if any such vehicle has already been registered by any other authority under any law for the time being in force or if such provisions for sanitary arrangement have already been made by any other local authority.

Sub-section (3) of section 55 says that the scale of fees or rates and the terms and conditions for the imposition thereof shall be such as may be provided under bye-laws.

(4) Such bye-laws may provide for exemption from all or any of the fees or rates in any class or cases. Section 56 of the Bihar Act prescribes that a Panchayat Samiti can raise loan or borrow money from the Government, banks or financial institutions; but for raising loan an borrowing from banks / FIs prior sanction of the State Government is necessary.

(5) Similarly, Section 82 of the Bihar Act authorizes the Zila Parishad to levy tolls in respect to ferry, fees on registration of boats and vehicles, for providing sanitary arrangements, licence fee for mela, lighting rate and water rate. Alike Panchayat Samiti, Zila Parishad has also been prohibited from levying fees on already registered vehicles or places where sanitary arrangement has already been made. Again, the fees or rates and terms and conditions for their imposition are to be provided by the bye laws.

Notwithstanding the provisions under section 27, 55 and 82 of the Bihar Panchayat Raj Act 1993/2006, it is clear that taxes could be imposed by the Panchayat Raj Bodies only when the State government frames rules, specifies maximum rates and provides bye-laws for tax imposition. Similarly the recommendations of the State Finance Commission, under Section 28, is not binding on the State Government.

Further, Panchayat Samiti and Zila Parishad can raise loans from public or borrow money from banks and other financial institutions only when the state government accords sanction to its proposal, as section 56 and 83 of the Act provide. Though the State government had transferred certain functions to Panchayats corresponding funds were yet to be transferred to Panchayats. Local mobilisation of funds remained a distant dream for Panchayats.

The Task Force constituted by the Union Government, after examining the issue of tax imposition suggested that State Legislature should legally prescribe it, instead of leaving it to be decided by the executive government. The Parliamentary Standing Committee in its 37th Report concurred with the Task Force, but keeping in view the federal character of polity restrained from prescribing any uniform standard. However, it exhorted the state legislature to utilize its discretionary powers to strengthen the finances of Panchayats by arrangement of certain revenue powers and sharing of state revenues with Panchayats and payment of Grant-in-aid.

The Parliamentary Standing Committee in its 37th Report (2002) recommended that the Union Government should make the earnest effort to persuade the State Legislatures to consider which of the taxes assigned to the Panchayats might be left to be appropriated by the Panchayats and request State Government to enact appropriate legislation in this regard.

Another important aspect as to the financial devolution related to the constitution of State Finance Commission (SFC) is mandated under Article 243 I, to review the financial position of Panchayats and make recommendations. Issues to be examined by SFC includes the principles that should govern the distribution between the State and Panchayats of the net proceeds of taxes, duties, tolls and fees leviable by the State. The allocation between Panchayats at all levels of their respective shares of such proceeds also comes under its purview. The SFC was also entrusted to determine the principles governing taxes, tolls, fees and duties that may be assigned to, or appropriated by the Panchayats; and also the grant-in-aid to the Panchayats from the Consolidated Fund of the State. It is also to suggest the measured needed to improve the financial position of the Panchayats.

The Bihar Act 1993 as well as 2006 under Article 168 provides for the Finance Commission for Panchayats. The provisions are similar to Article 243 I.

Inter-tier allocation of functions is one of the important dimensions of devolution. In order to ensure a balanced distribution of powers and functions between three tiers, a match between responsibility and authority provided is imperative.

An exhaustive analysis of activity mapping along functional distribution has been made hereunder. The following significant items have been taken up for detailed consideration:

1. Agriculture (including Horticulture) and Extension.
2. Animal Husbandry, Dairying and Poultry.
3. Fisheries.
4. Rural Housing (including Indira Awaas Yojana).
5. Drinking Water.
6. Roads, Culverts, Bridges etc.
7. Education including Primary and Secondary Schools.

Agriculture

Agriculture including extension is the first item in the

Eleventh Schedule. It has many aspects—increasing agricultural, horticultural and vegetable production; assessment and distribution of inputs, credit support, extension support, soil testing, post-harvest management, and risk management.

Regarding increase in production, Gram Panchayats have a role in estimation of crop yielding and maintenance of data base, in preparation of crop plan, in advising farmers about remunerative crop activities and crop diversification, in identifying progressive farmers for adoption and diffusion of new technologies, in providing customs hiring services for plant protection equipment and farm implements, and generating awareness in use of organic vermiculture, etc.

However, Panchayat Samitis could help in crop yields estimation through maintaining link with various agencies; assist Zila Parishads in organizing Kisan Mela, organizing on-farm verification trials and demonstration of new technologies, coordinating activities of VLWs and acting as a link between Zila Parishad and Gram Panchayats for transfer of knowledge and technologies.

As regards assessment and distribution of inputs, Gram Panchayats can assess the needs for various inputs such as seeds, fertilizers, pesticides, while the Panchayat Samiti can forward the consolidated need to the Zila Parishad. Similarly, Panchayat Samiti can ensure timely availability, storage and transport facilities for inputs, while Gram Panchayats can assist in timely distribution. Panchayat Samiti has to maintain close monitoring of inputs delivery system.

As regards credit support, Gram Panchayats can be instrumental in formation of self-help groups (SHGs), assessing credit needs, exercising social control in recovery of loans from credit institutions. Panchayat Samiti is to assist in credit plan preparation, ensuring timely credit from formal institutions and monitor credit delivery system. In

Bihar, Primary Agriculture Cooperative Societies (PACS), Regional Rural Banks and Nationalised Banks are primary source of formed credit support and they operate outside the scope of PRIs.

As regards assessment and distribution of inputs, Gram Panchayats can assess the needs for various inputs such as seeds, fertilizers, pesticides, while the Panchayat Samiti can forward the consolidated need to the Zila Parishad. Similarly, Panchayat Samiti can ensure timely availability, storage and transport facilities for inputs, while Gram Panchayats can assist in timely distribution. Panchayat Samiti has to maintain close monitoring of inputs delivery system.

As regards credit support, Gram Panchayats can be instrumental in formation of self-help groups (SHGs), assessing credit needs, exercising social control in recovery of loans from credit institutions. Panchayat Samiti is to assist in credit plan preparation, ensuring timely credit from formal institutions and monitor credit delivery system. In Bihar, Primary Agriculture Cooperative Societies (PACS), Regional Rural Banks and nationalised banks are primary source of formal credit support and they operate outside the scope of PRIs.

As regards extension support, Gram Panchayats identifies suitable plots for conducting trials end demonstration, selects farmers for participation in Krishi Mela and training programmes. While the Panchayati Samiti prepared plan and monitors the visit of extension workers to the villages. It ensures linkage between scientists and extension officials and farmers / Gram Panchayats.

As regards soil testing Panchayati Samiti helps in identifying locations for soil testing work, monitors soil testing work and helps farmers as per testing results. While the Gram Panchayat assists technicians in conducting soil tests, ensures feedback to farmers, selects beneficiaries for assistance and undertakes distribution of assistance.

Similarly in post-harvest management, Panchayat Samiti is to maintain godowns, regulate market charges, ensure correct weights and measures and also quick sale of products and payment to farmers. Gram Panchayat is to assist in increasing awareness about storage facility and organize farmers for group sale of produce.

In Risk management, Gram Panchayats have a more significant role in reporting of losses due to natural calamities and rehabilitation requirements; supervision of relief operations and distribution of materials; motivating farmers for taking crop insurance schemes; and in the implementation of contingency plan. However, the Panchayat Samiti has a role in identifying farmers for crop insurance scheme and in providing benefits to farmers. It also has a role in estimating crop losses and monitoring relief operations.

But at the ground level, Gram Panchayats play only the role of facilitator to the Block Development Officer and/or Block Agriculture Extension Officer, when they have to distribute some inputs or to make farmers aware of any scheme they call Mukhiyas. Agriculture Extension Officers exercise control over VLWs. Gram Panchayats or the Panchayat Samiti seldom initiates activities on its own, as they do not have resources. Though, the VLW attends the meeting of Gram Sabha. A Mukhiya of Paroo block from 2001 to 2006 reported in an informal interview with the researcher that all the functions listed in the Constitution and the Act are seldom performed by the Gram Panchayats.

So far as the Panchayat Samiti is concerned, the only agricultural farm in Paroo block is at Deoria which is in depilated condition. It is used by adjoining villagers as grazing ground for their cattle. Panchayat Samiti does not own it; it is the property of the state government's Department of Agriculture. The farm remained uncultivated and the BAO could not explain its reasons. The functional visibility of Panchayat Samiti in the eyes of people was limited to the distribution of seeds of rice and oilseeds that was provided by the State Government.

VLWs report to the BAO, who in return reports to DAO. The BAO attends Panchayat Samiti meetings and other meetings called by the Pramukh. Similarly, the DAO attends Zila Parishad meetings, reports to it. But the DAO is accountable to the State Government and the District Magistrate.

So devolution of functions and activity mapping exercises have little impact on the hierarchic departmental structure. Thus the lack of devolution of funds and functionaries impedes the proper implementation of the devolution scheme in terms of functions also.

2. Animal Husbandry, Dairying and Poultry is the second item. It has five aspects – development of livestock; veterinary services; feeding and fodder including support during droughts; dairy development; and poultry development.

As regards development of livestock, Gram Panchayats have a limited role to assist in identification of beneficiaries under various programmes and motivate people to maintain quality bread and modern methods of livestock maintenance. Distribution of quality breed to beneficiaries and propagation of improved bread come within the purview of Panchayat Samiti.

As regards veterinary services, Gram Panchayats have to supervise the functioning of Rural Livestock Units, and Artificial Insemenisation (AI) centres and to report outbreak of diseases and epidemics, while supervising the overall functioning of veterinary services and maintaining mobile veterinary unit come within the purview of the Panchayat Samiti.

As regards feeding and fodder, Gram Panchayats have to help in establishing cooperative fodder farm, allocation of community land for fodder production; to control grazing and improvement in grazing and pasture lands; and selection of beneficiaries and distribution of fodder during droughts. However, community land is not owned by Gram Panchayats. Panchayat Samitis have to organise cooperatives for fodder production and provide financial assistances; to supply improved variety of fodder seeds; to provide modern methods of feeding to improve livestock productivity; and to supply of fodder during droughts to the Gram Panchayats.

As regards dairy development, Gram Panchayats' supposed area of activity include organizing milk producers' cooperatives, establishing milk collection centres and identification of beneficiaries for dairy development programme. However, Panchayat Samiti is to encourage milk producers cooperative societies, to ensure timely payment to the milk producers and to supply to quality milch animals to the Gram Panchayats. At the ground level, Tirhut Milk Utpadan Cooperative Ltd. (TIMUL) is organizing milk producers' cooperative societies, establishing milk collection centres, ensures timely payment to producers and provides cattle feed to them at reasonable price. TIMUL is an autonomous organization, works under the umbrella of State-level milk cooperative federation and presently has no structural-functional relation with the PRIs.

As regards poultry farming, identification of beneficiaries for poultry farming and allotting/leasing community land for establishing poultry complex are the identified activities of Gram Panchayats, while the Panchayat Samiti has to arrange for the supply of poultry feed and to assist in establishing poultry complex for them under various programmes. On the ground level, Panchayat Samiti and Gram Panchayats merely popularises government schemes and often organises awareness camps about them.

Veterinary doctor at the block level is the only visible symbol of the animal husbandry department. Some trained rural folk with necessary equipments, medicines etc. have been made available in rural area for assisting farmers. They receive assistance and incentive out of government funds. Panchayat Samiti has distributed a few milch cows to identified beneficiaries drawn from scheduled caste people.

Fisheries are the next item. It has aspects such as inland fisheries, developing of marketing / processing infrastructure and welfare measures. Gram Panchayats have to develop village ponds for fisheries; leasing ponds to Fishermen cooperative groups; identification of beneficiaries for assistance; assisting Panchayat Samiti in the distribution of boats, nets and other materials; and supervision and reporting progress to the Panchayati Samiti. In fact, government ponds are still auctioned by the Circle Officers and the collected revenue is credited into government treasury.

However, Gram Panchayats are spending money in renovation of ponds out of National Rural Employment Guarantee Scheme funds.

Panchayat Samiti also executes fish pond improvement projects. It selects fisherman for training. A good number of fishermen were sent to Andhra Pradesh for training. It distributes boats, nets, tools etc. to the fishermen cooperatives. It monitors the activities of Gram Panchayats and sends report to the Zila Parishad. Fisheries Extension Supervisors are the functionaries entrusted with this task, but many blocks do not have this functionary. One supervisor looks after many blocks.

PRIs have role in development of marketing and processing infrastructure for fisheries and also in welfare measures for fishermen. Gram Panchayats are to establish these infrastructures and Panchayat Samiti is to organise training in processing, packaging and preservation and to develop tag-up arrangements between fishermen and the processing units. Similarly, implementation of family/group insurance schemes for fishermen and distribution of relief to the families affected by calamity come under the purview of Panchayati Samiti. Gram Panchayats are to encourage them to take up insurance schemes, to assess loss/damage and relief requirement; and to select beneficiaries.

Rural Housing is one of the major functional areas assigned to the PRIs. Gram Sabha is to select beneficiaries for Indira Awaas Yojana. Gram Panchayat is to assist in allotment / distribution of house sites to landless families. Providing assistance in procuring building materials, particularly bricks, has emerged as on onerous task in view of paucity of brick kilns and low government rate in the face of rise in market price.

Panchayati Samiti compiles the beneficiary lists. Complaints of corruption in rural housing schemes are rampant. PRIs have the power to supervise construction in terms of quality of work, use of materials. Junior Engineers assist the Panchayati Samiti and the Gram Panchayat, however complaints of harassment and bribery surface. All the rural housing schemes are either centrally sponsored or out of the backward region grant fund.

As regards drinking water, Gram Panchayat receive fund out of Bharat Nirman schemes. They identify schemes and location, estimate costs and formulate projects through the involvement of the Gram Sabha. Panchayat Samiti identifies and priorities villages, seeks technical assistance from the PHED engineers. A parallel committee is functional at district level that is called Prakalp. It awards drinking water and sanitary scheme implementation and maintenance tasks to various NGOs bypassing the PRIs. Zila Parishad Chairperson and the DDC along with PHED executive engineer play main role in it. These NGOs seek formal / informal cooperation with the PRIs.

Construction and maintenance of rural Roads, culverts and bridges is one of the major tasks of PRIs. That they perform mostly out of the centrally sponsored schemes. Gram

Sabha is to be involved in approving road construction projects, while technical assistance is to be provided by the Panchayat Samiti engineers. Panchayati Samiti also takes up link road construction projects. Funds for road construction are available, but quality of work is overlooked as the vigilance committees seldom delve deep into it.

Primary Education is one of the main tasks of the Panchayat Samiti and Gram Panchayats is which PRIs have come to play major role since last two years. Gram Panchayats play role not only in ensuring full enrolment of school age children; maintenance of school buildings, play grounds; vigilance to regulate teachers' attendance and distribution of study materials, but of late they have also selected and appointed primary teachers. In Bihar the powers to appoint teachers for primary, middle, secondary and senior secondary schools were given to the urban and rural local bodies. Zila Parishads selected and appointed teachers of secondary and senior secondary schools and posted them against sanctioned vacant posts within the district; while Panchayat Samiti selected and appointed teachers for middle schools, they were posted in schools within the block. Gram Panchayats selected teachers for primary schools. These newly appointed teachers were issued appointed letters by the CEO of Zila Parishad, EO of Panchayat Samiti and Secretary of Gram Panchayat Panchayats (previously called Panchayat Sevak). Former Shiksha Mitras were also designated as Panchayat Shikshak, provided they possess necessary minimum qualification. These teachers receive salary out of state government grant. Gram Panchayats play major role in maintenance, up gradation and construction of primary school buildings.

To ensure full enrolment of school age children and their retention in schools remained an onerous task for Gram Panchayats. Every primary school is managed by a School Education Committee. This committee is formed through election. Mukhiya of the Gram Panchayat nominates two members into each committee.

In addition to be centrally sponsored schemes, the GOI has introduced R.S.V.Y and B. R. G. F. schemes as relatively untied grants. Relatively untied grants mean that though some priority areas have been indicated, Panchayats themselves could determine their own priorities and the allocations they would be making among competing demands. The state governments have to certify that the money from earlier instalments have in fact reached Panchayats. Bihar is also tardy in applying for and securing its instalment in due time, though it has not delayed disbursal to the PRIs, MoPR is opposed to state's move in giving MLAs any voice in determining the Twelve Finance Commission grants. One drawback is that there is neither any compulsion for State Finance Commission recommendations being accepted nor any statutory timeliness for these to be acted upon.

A sum of Rs. 3750 crore for 2006-2007 was placed at the disposal of MoPR to administer the BRGF scheme. Budget provision for 2007-2008 was to rise to Rs. 4400 crore. BRGF grants are untied. Panchayats are expected to use these grants for gap filling in existing development programme to build the development infrastructure in such a manner as to promote the closing of the gap between backward and non-backward districts. Districts receive about 10 to 15 crore in a year.

The thrust of the Ministry of Panchayati Raj is that functions, functionaries and finances to PRIs are suitable devolved to empower Gram Sabhas and District Planning Committees to make Panchayati Raj Institutions true institutions of self government. But the states are not following its suggestions. Bihar has not adopted as yet fund transfer monitoring software developed by the Ministry of Panchayat Raj. Bihar could not provide data on PRI wise Twelfth Finance Commission grants released as on 1st

February 2008.[7]

To institutionalise the system of Panchayati Raj Institutions and make it most representative and participatory remains the challenge even today. In terms of devolution, three priority areas for immediate concerted action are activity maps, Panchayat Sector windows in State budgets and assignment of the functionaries. The first is related to functions. Activity mapping in the indispensable need for the preparation of detailed spelling out of activities with respect to each devolved function so that there is no ambiguity at any level about the tasks entrusted to them or any overlapping of duties. Secondly, Panchayat Sector window in the state budget means insertion of an appropriate budget line in the budgets of relevant line departments of the state government to ensure the flow of funds for undertaking devolved activities to the Panchayats at the level of the PRI to which any given activity has been assigned in the Activity Map. This has to be done in conformity with the pattern of devolution of functions. It is related to funds. Third is the assignment of functionaries in conformity with the pattern of devolution of functions and finances to that level of the Panchayati Raj System to which any given activity in the Active Map. Activity mapping at the level of various ministries of Union government is the first task. As the central government funding through Central Sector and centrally sponsored schemes is the main source of PRIs receipts. The new schemes such as the Backward Regions Grant Fund, National Rural Employment Guarantee Schemes spell out the specific duties of the Panchayats at each level with respect the programmes.

The Rural Electrification policy—the Rajiv Gandhi Vidyutikaran Yojana, the National Rural Health Mission and the Jan Kerosene Yojana have a significant Panchayati Raj component. Many previous schemes have been amended. These schemes are the Sarva Shiksha Abhiyan, the Mid-Day

Meal Scheme, the National Literary Mission, the Rajiv Gandhi Drinking Water Mission and Total Sanitation Campaign.[8]

The steps to devolve functions in relation to the Integrated Child Development Scheme (ICDS), other schemes of Ministry of Social Justice and Empowerment are also underway.

As regards the Bharat Nirman programmes, the Finance Minister in his budget speech (2005-2006) had underlined the centrality of the Panchayats in its success. Disaster Management is an area where Panchayats can play a major role.

The union government is favouring the "Big Bang" approach. It means placing confidence in Panchayats and substantially devolving functions in one giant step instead of incremental movement towards more devolution. The Gram Panchayat Swaraj Yojana aims at it as the scheme provides funds for capacity building and undertaking formal training exercises. It is imperative on the part of State governments to devolve the planning function to the PRIs because of the insistence on District Planning for release of funds under Backward Regions Grant Fund. District Planning Committee has been constituted in Bihar.

The Government of India insists that moneys meant for Panchayats should reach them without delay or diversion. That is why the Twelve Finance Commission (2005-10) has set aside Rupees 20000/- crore largely in the form of relatively united grants to be directed to the PRIs.

The Government of India holds that provisions for basic infrastructure for all the Panchayats is required to be made by the State Governments. To supplement the efforts of the State governments, Ministry of Panchayati Raj under Rashtriya Gram Swaraj Yojana (RGSY) for construction and up gradation of the Panchayat Ghars provides Rupees 10.15

crore and Rs. 16.22 crore in 2006-2007 and 2007-2008 respectively. Under the Backward Regions Grants Fund (BRGF) scheme, Rs. 1.00 crore per district is earmarked for capacity building of Panchayats. The capacity building in this case includes office infrastructure, office building connectivity to these offices through roads, telephones, e-connectivity, Power supply etc.[9]

Before BRGF scheme, there was a scheme of the Planning Commission called Rashtriya Sam Vikas Yojana under Backward Districts Initiative. Under this scheme, total amount to be released to Muzaffarpur district was Rs. 45 crore. Out of the above amount three instalments of Rs. 7.5 crores were released to the district during 2005-06, 06-07 and 07-08 respectively. In fact, only 50% amount was released to the district. No amount was released during 2003-04 and 04-05.[10]

Further regarding devolution, it was also reported to the Lok Sabha that 25 subjects have been transferred through legislation in Bihar and 25 subjects have been covered under Activity Mapping. A state government committee under Principal Secretary is looking at activity Mapping.

Under Rashtriya Gram Swaraj Yojana, Rs.4.39 crore was released to the State during 2006-2007, while under capacity building scheme Rs.14.46 crore was released during 2006-2007.[11]

Conclusion

It has been accepted beyond doubt that not bureaucratic development but participative development through grassroots democracy is the imperative need. The scheme outlined in Part IX contains the key to inclusive growth through inclusive governance. It has been realised by policy makers that inclusive growth could be achieved only through participative development.

It has been realised that the empowerment of Panchayat Raj Institutions has been uneven, fitful and subject to reversal in many states. This is inevitable because the Constitution leaves it exclusively within the diction of the state to determine the nature, direction and pace of devolution.

However, the union government could greatly accelerate and rationalise the devolution within the present constitutional scheme as well. The principal source of funding for Panchayati Raj Institutions is the centrally sponsored schemes. If the union government adapts the guidelines of these schemes to ensure centrality of PRIs in the planning and implementation of these schemes in conformity with the letter and spirit of Part IX and Eleventh Schedule, the scenario could change. Ministry of Panchayati Raj has taken initiative in this regard.

The Ministry of Panchayati Raj has started giving incentive to states. It has launched Panchayat Empowerment and Accountability Incentivisation Scheme (PEAIS) through which it awards states and panchayats doing well in terms of various transparency and accountability indices. Eleventh five year plan document accepts the need to build in incentives that would encourage the states to devolve functions, funds and functionaries to the PRIs. The ministry is seeking support from International Development Association through the World Bank for the scheme.

It is hoped that the Thirteenth Finance Commission would consider increasing block untied non-plan grants to Panchayats. So that the PRIs have an adequate reservoir of financial resources which could be used for the maintenance of community assets and improved service delivery. Then the PRIs could plan and implement schemes for neighbourhood economic development and social justice.

References

1. In National Common Minimum Programme of the United Progressive Alliance, New Delhi, 2004

2. 37th Report, 2002, Lok Sabha Secretariat, New Delhi

3. See, Appendix-V of the 37th Report, p. 111-112

4. Report of the Task Force to operationalise administrative decentralization of funds, functions and functionaries upon Panchayats, 2001, Ministry of Rural Development, New Delhi, Annexure – III, p. 1002

5. Ibid, Annexure IV, P. 1003.

6. 37th Report, Appendix VI, pp. 113-177

7. State of Panchayats, Vol. III, Annexure 20, MoPR, New Delhi, 2008

8. Mani Shankar Aiyar, Overview : Panchayati Raj in India-The Greatest Experiment in Democracy Ever, MoPR, N. Delhi, 2007,p. 5

9. Lok Sabha Questions, Unstarred no. 5128 dated April 30, 2008, reply by Mani Shankar Aiyar, Minister, website *www.loksabha.nic.in* accessed on 14 September 2008.

10. Lok Sabha Starred Questions Number 102, answered on 5 March 2008, Lok Sabha Website accessed on 14.9.2008

11. Lok Sabha, Starred Questions No. 118 dated 5.3.2008, Lok Sabha Website, accessed on 14.9.2008

4

Working of Panchayati Raj Institutions- An Appraisal of Paroo Block

The purpose of this chapter is to present an appraisal of the working of the Panchayati Raj Institutions in the Paroo block of Muzaffarpur district in Bihar. For the collection of primary data field studies were carried out within the Paroo block area. Separate questionnaires were operationalised among eighteen categories of respondents. Altogether 30 questions were asked. In certain categories respondents were selected through sampling method. This sampling method was applied in selecting respondents from among elected Gram Panchayat and Panchayat Samiti functionaries, Gram Panchayat Panchayat Secretaries and members of general public who constitute the Gram Panchayat Sabha. Broad Questions were framed in order to elicit factual information about the working of the Gram Panchayat Sabha, Gram Panchayat Panchayat, Panchayat Samiti and its various committees. These questions covered almost all aspects listed in the problem of this research work. Questions were so framed as to facilitate identification of some meaningful their persistent recurrence.

In addition to the questionnaires, other methods of empirical data collection were also relied upon that included conducting structured and unstructured open ended interviews with the Block Development Officer who also functions as the Secretary of the Panchayat Samiti; the Chair person of the Zila Parishad; the Deputy Development Commissioner who is the chief executive officer of the Zila Parishad; the District Panchayat Raj Officer and also with the journalists of popular widely circulated Hindi Newspaper – *Aaj, Dainik Jagaran* and *Hindustan* based at the block level. Further, interview was also conducted with the elected Zila Parishad members from the block area, teachers, Nayaya Panchayat functionaries and former elected three-tier Panchayat functionaries etc. while randomly selecting respondents from general public due caution was given to make the sample representative enough so as to include proportionate voice from Women, Scheduled Castes, Farmers, Housewives, College students, educated youth etc.

Relevant reports in newspapers about the working of Panchayat Raj Institutions in Paroo block were also scanned for the purpose. The researcher had the benefit of being in the faculty of a college situated in the same area. The researcher's additional assignment as the programme officer of the National Service Scheme at the college provided ample opportunities to work among the villagers. It facilitated observation from close quarters very near to participant observation. The researcher was conscious to remain objective during the data collection, data processing and data analyses processes.

This work was aimed at testing the following hypotheses :

1. Rural scenario in Bihar, particularly its power structure; witnessed major change due to the new Panchayat Raj Institutions.

2. A leadership change has occurred in the rural area,

particularly in terms of caste, class, gender, age and occupation.

3. Elected Panchayat functionaries from women, scheduled castes and extremely backward castes, though in fair number due to reservation, still face challenge and impediments. They are yet to acquire the actual leadership role and position.

4. Devolution of functions, funds and functionaries is inadequate.

5. Gram Panchayat Sabha is yet to become a genuine mode of participatory democracy.

Theoretically, this work begun with the premise that the PRIs represent decentralisation, participation, responsiveness, legitimacy and liberty. The PRIs have decentralisation combined with democratisation that may provide greater transparency, accountability, responsiveness, probity, frugality, efficiency, equity and opportunities for mass participation. This work premised that participation makes better citizens and increasing disenchantment with indirect democracy would make participatory democracy attractive to the masses.

While appraising the working of Panchayat Raj Institutions in Paroo block in order to test the above hypotheses framed on the basis of the above theoretical premises, answers were searched to questions that have emerged during preliminary work on this problem. These questions ranged from the expected role of Gram Sabha as a regulator of key institutions and its impact on minimisation of bureaucratic power to the social sensitisation and attitudinal changes towards elected members and office holders from women, scheduled castes and extremely backward castes. These questions included the correlation between written powers and functions and the actual administrative, technical and functional support to exercise those powers and to discharge those functions. The impact of overlapping functions between

Gram Panchayat and Panchayat Samiti on the working was also sought to be ganged.

The expanse of the research work was limited to the Paroo block of Muzaffarpur district in Bihar field data collection but if was always hoped that the conclusions drawn could be easily generalised on the new Panchayat Raj System in Bihar. The repeal of 1993 Act with a new Act in 2006 provided an opportunity to underline distinctive differences between the 2001 and 2006 PRIs structure in Bihar.

Locale

The district of Muzaffarpur forms part of the North Bihar plains. It is located centrally in Tirhut Division of Bihar State. The old Muzaffarpur district was created during British period by splitting up the earlier district of Tirhut in the year 1875. After formation of Sitamarhi and Vaishali districts in the year 1972, the new Muzaffarpur district is constituted of the old Sadan sub-division. The present Sitamarhi and Vaishali districts were earlier the subdivisions of the Muzaffarpur district created in 1875. At present the district has two sub divisions – Muzaffarpur East and Muzaffarpur West consisting of 9 and 7 development blocks respectively. Muzaffarpur East subdivision has Musahari, Minapur, Bochahan, Bandara, Aurai, Katra, Gaighatti, Moraul and Sakra blocks. Muzaffarpur West has Kurhani, Kanti, Saraiya, Paroo, Sahebganj and Baruraj blocks under it. Thus the Paroo block is among the seven blocks of Muzaffarpur West sub-division. As stated earlier, every development block has a Panchayat Simiti consisting of 47 members elected from territorial constituencies. At present there are 34 Gram Panchayats in the Paroo block.

Before presenting an appraisal, if is imperative to look as the evolution of PRIs. According to the District Gazetteer of Muzaffarpur, the Bihar Panchayat Raj Act 1947 (Act VII of 1948) was actually implemented in the district of Muzaffarpur on the 15th January 1949. the scheme aimed at the establishment of local self-government in every nook and corner of the state and also decentralisation of power.

The Muzaffarpur District Gazetteer of 1957 states that the Panchayat Raj system intended to make people conscious to share the responsibility in matters of social and economic uplift of the village community. The Gram Panchayat were vested with the executive and judicial powers along with powers to raise taxes for their local needs. Improvement in communications, irrigation, education, public health and village industries were the important functions of Gram Panchayats under the 1947 Act.

The Government had provided a Gram Sevak in each Gram Panchayat who after receiving proper training acted as an agent for execution of development schemes and to carry on the office work in the Gram Kuchery. Mukhia of Gram Panchayat was an honorary chief officer elected by the members of the village Panchayat. It was to be reported to the District Panchayat Raj Officer. Prior to 1993, there was no state Election Commission to conduct these elections. During late 1940s and 1950s there existed informality in the structure of village panchayats as evident from the Muzaffarpur District Gazetteer of 1957 (p.112).

The District had 262 notified Gram Panchayats in 1951. Basides these, there were 121 non-official Panchayats functioning the district. The proposed number of Gram Panchayats, under the 1947 Act, was 809. The picture in 1957 is given below :-

Muzaffarpur District : Gram Panchayats in 1957

1. Total number of Gram Panchayats —— 739.
2. Total number of official Gram Panchayats —— 501.
3. Total number of unofficial Gram Panchayats — 238.
4. Total number of villages covered by notified Gram Panchayats-3269.

5. Total number of villages covered by un-official Gram Panchayats-1171.

The Muzaffarpur District Gazetter (1957) notes that within a few years of their existence the Gram Panchayats were able to execute a number of projects particularly some important embankments besides village roads. It is stated in the Gazetteer that to make any objective appraisal of the Gram Panchayats so soon would have been premature, but it said that they have had good response from the villagers who have become conscious of the good work that could be done through the Gram Panchayats.

Extracting extensively from the Muzaffarpur District Gazetteer of 1957 was intended to provide background for proper appreciation of the transformation ushered in through the constitutional Amendment in early 1990s. First election to the three-tier Panchayat Raj Institutions under the Bihar Panchayat Raj Act 1993 was held in 2001 when there were 34 Gram Panchayats in the Paroo block. Prior to those elections for Panchayat Raj Institutions, these were held in 1978 when there were only 22 Gram Panchayats in the Paroo block.

A list of twenty two, Gram Panchayats that existed in 1978 in being given below :-

(i) Dharfari,

(ii) Mohabbatpur

(iii) Neknampur

(iv) Utsi

(v) Pandeh

(vi) Baijalpur

(vii) Khutahi

(viii) Gyaspur

(ix) Fatehabad

(x) Jaimal Dumri

(xi) Kamalpura

(xii) Paroo (South)

(xiii) Paroo (North)

(xiv) Bahaddinpur

(xv) Mohjamma

(xvi) Anandpur Kharauni

(xvii) Deoria

(xviii) Saraiya

(xix) Cochanhi Chapra

(xx) Bajitpur

(xxi) Lalu Chapra and

(xxii) Raghunathpur.

The elections in 1978 were held under BPR Act 1947 which did not provide for resonation. None of the Mukhias elected in 1978 was a woman. None from the scheduled castes was elected to the past. Only three Mukhias belonged to the numerous other backward castes. They were elected from Mohabbatpur, Saraiyya and Raghunathpur Gram Panchayats. 19 out of 22 Mukhiya belonged to the upper castes. Among the upper castes Bhumihar caste had 12 representatives, while Rajputs had 3, Brahmins 2 and Kayastha 3 representatives.

From the standpoint of the study, a comparison between the social composition of Mukhiya elected in 1978 and 2001 becomes important as an indicator of changing social profile of rural leadership. Though for the past of chairperson of a Gram Panchayat (Mukhiya) there was no reservation in accordance with the Patna High Court order of 1996 discussed in chapter 1. But out of 34 Mukhia elected in 2001, 21 belonged to the non-upper castes. Only 13 belonged to the upper castes.

The scheduled castes remain un-represented. Gender wise, none of the Mukhia was an women. By 2001, 12 new Gram Panchayats were created as per the requirements of the 1993 Act. These Gram Panchayats are :-

Chandkewari, Kataru, Chakki Sohagpur, Chintamanpur, Jafarpur, Bishunpur Saraiyya, Magurahiaya, Jagdishpur, Kauria Nijamat, Rampur Kesho, Malahi and Bhagwanpur Simra. The existing Deoria Gram Panchayat was divided into Deoria (East) and Deoriea (West). Out of 21 non-upper caste Mukhias elected in 2001, 9 of them belonged to the Yadav caste. Extremely backward castes also saw an increase in their representation in an open election. While in 1978 there representation was only one, it rose to three in 2001, all of them belonged to the Sahni community. They were elected from Fatehabad, Chochanhi Chapra and Raghunathpur Panchayats. Three contestants from the religions minority, Muslim community were also elected in 2001. Among the OBCs, two from Kurmiand Koeri and one each from Kalwar and Teli were elected.

As discussed in Chapter-1 and Chapter-2, reservation from women, scheduled castes and extremely backward castes was introduced for the posts of chairpersons during 2006 elections to the Panchayati Raj Institutions. Thus out of 34 Gram Panchayats, 17 posts of chair persons (Mukhias) were reserved for women. The break-up of reservation for 17 women Mukhia posts in given below :- General-12, EBC-3 and SC-2. However, Six out of 12 Women General seats of Mukhia went to upper caste Bhumihars and three to Rajputs. Outher three women General Mukhia seats went one act to Muslim, Yadav and Kurni contestants. It is pertinent to note that benefit of reservation was not available to the relatively well-off other backward castes placed in Annexure-II of the Bihar List. Among others Yadav, Kurmi, Koeri, Tele etc. belong to the Annexure-I category mentioned above.

As regards the 17 Mukhia seats not reserved exclusively for women, 3 were reserved for SC and 4 for the EBG, leaving only 10 seats open to all contestants. Thus the reservation breaking of 34 Mukhia seats in 2006 emerges as: General open 10, EBC open 4 and SC open 3, and women general 12, EBC women 3 and SC women 2. So, for EBCs seven and for SCs 5 seats were reserved, leaving 22 seats open and women seats for general candidates. This reservation structure altered the social composition of Mukhia elected in 2006. The table below gives its complete picture.

Table – 1

Name	*Number*
EBC Open	4
Kanu	2
EBC Women	-
Kumhar	3
SC Women	2
SC Open	3
General Women	12
Bhumihar	6
Rajput	3
OBC (Yadav, Kurmi)	2
General Open	1
Rajput	1
OBC Kurmi	1
Yadav	4
EBC Kanu	1
Nai	1

Thus two extremely backward castes candidates were elected from the open general seats. So, the number of upper castes got reduced to 12 in which 9 were women elected from reserved seats.

Table – 2

Changing social profile of rural leadership : A comparative picture of Mukhias elected in 1978, 2001 and 2006 in Paroo block.

Social category	Gender	1978	2001	2006
Scheduled Castes	Men	×	×	3
	Women	×	×	2
Extremely Backward Castes	Men	1	3	6
	Women	×	×	3
Other Backward Castes	Men	2	15	5
	Women	×	×	2
Muslim	Men	×	3	×
	Women	×	×	1
Upper Casts	Men	19	13	3
	Women	×	×	9

(*Source:* Data computed on the basis of election results and field studies)

Similar transfermation in the social composition of rural leadership was reflected from the list of members elected for the Panchayat Samiti – the intermediate tier of the three-tier Panchayat Raj structure as also in the list of Gram Panchayat ward members, sarpanch, Panches and Zila Parishad members elected from Paroo block.

Total elective seats of Panchayat Samiti members was 47 in which 23 women were reserved for women candidates. However 24 women were elected to the Panchayat Samiti. Interestingly a women from the reserved extremely backward caste Nonia community was elected from the general women seats. Only five seates were reserved for EBC women but they won six seats. Three Muslim women were also elected.

The table below presents a glimpse of social profile of Panchayat Samiti members elected in 2006.

Table – 3

Panchayat Samiti Members (47) of Paroo Block

Social Category	Gender	Sub Categories				
Upper Castes-12	Men-4 Women-8				Bhumihar- 3 4	Rajput- 1 4
OBC-7	Mem-4 Women-3			Yadav 1 3	Koeri 1 ×	Kalwar 2 ×
OBC-14	Mem-8 Women-6	Nonia-2 1 1	Malah-5 2 3	Kanu-5 3 2	Gorh-1 1 ×	Kumhar- 1 ×
SC-11	Mem-7 Women-4				Ravidas 5 2	Paswan 2 2
Muslim-3	Mem-0 Women-3	× 3				

(Source : Computed on the basis of election results and field studies)

Similar representative character was reflected in the list of Sarpanches who head the nayaya panchayat of Gram Panchayat Panchayat level out of 17 women seats, 10 were general, while five and two seats were reserved respectively for the extremely backward castes and the scheduled castes respectively.

Table below depicts the social composition of Sarpanches elected in 2006.

Table – 4

Social Category	Gender	Sub Category					
Scheduled Castes 5					Ram	Sweeper	Paswan
	Men-3				2	1	×
	Women-2				1	×	×
Extremely Backward Castes 9		Malah	Kanu	Nai	Jatwa	Nania	Chandwary
	Men-4	×	1	1	×	1	1
	Women-5	1	1	1	1	×	1
OBC 17					Yadav	Kurmi	Koeri
	Men-5				1	1	1
	Women-2				3	1	×
Upper Castes 13					Bramhan	Bhumihar	Rajput
	Men-5				1	2	2
	Women-8				×	6	2

(Source : Computed on the basis of field studies.)

So, for as the members of the Gram Panchayat is concerned, their total member is 466. They are elected from the territorial constituencies, called wards, demarcated in every Gram Panchayat. The number of wards in a Gram Panchayat ranges from 12 to 17. Due to the provision of reservation, their social composition also reflect similar trend. However, educationally and economically ward members represent the lower rung of the society.

Questionnaires were operationalised among various

categories of sampled respondents. Their responses to similar questions varied significantly. All the seven Mukhia respondents replied that they regularly convene Gram Sabha meetings. Vigilance Committed have been constituted in their Gram Panchayats. Office of the Gram Panchayat is situated in the Panchayat Bhawan. They give proper notice about the Gram Sabha meetings as also through beating of drums. They claimed that they convene Gram Panchayat executive committee meeting every two months. Mukhias reported that only the Panchayat Secretaries attend Gram Panchayat executive officer. No other government servant attends Gram Panchayat executive committee meetings. Between 2001 and 2006, no such occasion arose in any Gram Panchayat when Gram Panchayat executive committee meeting had to he reguisitioned by the ward members under section 20(2) and 20(5).

As regards the postponement of Gram Sabha meetings for want of quorum, the replies of Mukhias were vague. However between 2001 and 2006, most of the resolutions were passed in the re-convened meeting after adjournment, as no quorum was required for such a meeting. After 2006, section 5 was changed which mandated that attendance of one fortieth of the total number would suffice for quorum re-convened meeting. In most cases signatures are obtained after the meeting.

An interesting question put to the respondent Mukhias was related to chairing of Gram Panchayat executive committee meeting by a member other than Mukhia under section 21 (4). In none of the Panchayats such as occasion had ever arisen. This provision was put in the Act to ensure impartiality when in the aye of any member in the Act to ensure impartiality when in the eye of any member an issue, in which personal or financial interest of the Mukhia, has to be deliberated upon. As regards, devolution of functions to the Gram Panchayats most of the Mukhias (2001-2006) were unable to present any such list. Orally they conceded that functions have been devolved, but complained of lack of autonomy to the elected functionaries.

The Bihar Panchayat Raj Act 1993 as also BPR Act 2006 provides for assignment of certain functions by the Government to the Gram Panchayats. Under section 23, the Government may transfer the management and maintenance of a forest, waste lands, pasture lands, vacant lands, entrust the collection of land revenue and the maintenance of land records etc. when the attention of respondent Mukhias were drawn to this provision, they replied in affirmative that functions have been assigned. But when specifically asked to state concrete situation, they maintained that no such assignment has been made.

As to the constitution of the six standing committees of (a) planning, coordination and finance, (b) production, (c) social justice, (d) education, (e) public health, family welfare and rural sanitation and (f) public works under section 25, the respondent Mukhias accepted that no such standing committees has been constituted. Similarly, the Mukhias replied in negative about property and funds of the Gram Panchayat under section 26. Mukhias were asked as to whether Gram Panchayats have been given powers to impose taxes, fees and rates as specified under section 27 of the PPR Act 1993/2006. One of them replied that through a government letter issued in 2004 they were asked to impose taxes on occupants of holdings and also on professions etc. The Mukhias of Paroo block informally met and resolved that tax imposition in impractical. Six other respondent Mukhias said that tax imposition powers are not unavailable to Gram Panchayats.

As regards allocation of funds to Panchayats on the basis of State Finance Commission recommendations onwards 2001, Mukhias were reluctant to provide year-wise data. But they replied in affirmative. They accepted that funds have been regularly provided but whether under section 28 or not, they were not clear.

The respondent Mukhias stated that Gram Panchayats prepare their annual budget and get it passed by the Gram Panchayat executive committee. As regards the passage of budget by the Gram Sabha, Mukhias replied were ambiguous. The respondent Mukhias reported that regular audit of Gram Panchayat accounts has been done since 2001, but they were reluctant to provide a copy of the audit reports, instead they suggested that the office of the District Magistrate may be consulted for audit reports.

Village volunteer Force called Gram Raksha Dal for general watch and ward, and for meeting emergent events like fire, flood, breach of embankment, collapse of bridge, out break of epidemic, to encounter burglary or docoity and maintenance of public peace and order has to be constituted for every Gram Panchayat.

Respondent Mukhias reported that the Gram Raksha Dal is not constituted in their Gram Panchayat. Six out of seven respondent Mukhias belonged to a political party. Only one of them was a social worker having no party affiliation. As regards the previous occupation of respondent Mukhias, one among the seven was a businessman; another was an ex-serviceman, yet another was an assistant teacher; while four were farmers. As regards appointment, transfer and posting of secretaries of Gram Panchayats, it was done by the District Magistrate and his subordinate officers whom he has delegated the power.

As regards socio-political impact of the new Panchayat system on the rural society, five questions were put before the respondent Mukhias. These question were related to the (i) changes witnessed in village scenario, (ii) changes witnessed in rural power structure, (iii) functional autonomy in real terms, available to elected women members and office holders; (iv) change in the states of women; and (v) change in the social system – family particularly with reference to the position of women. All the seven respondent Mukhias reiterated a positive note. In open-ended interview, they narrated it with several concrete examples.

Another questionnaire was put before the members of the Panchayat Samiti. Questions were related to the working of the Panchayat Samiti. Out of 47 members, ten were selected as sample respondents. Three out of ten were women. Socially, only one belonged to upper caste Rajput. Two were from the scheduled castes, that too from two different communities – Ravidas and Washerman. One was a Muslim, others were from the backward castes – two each from the Yadav and Koeri communities, one each from extremely backward Kahar and relatively well off Bania communities. Economically, only one among them could be said to belong to a below poverty line family. Among the respondents only he was landless, others were landholders though marginal. Table below shows the socio-economic profile of the ten respondents from the 47 Panchayat Samiti Members.

Table - 5

Sr. No	Gender	Age	Education	Social	Caste
R_1	F	50	7th Class	SC	Ram
R_2	M	42	BA	SC	Dhobi
R_3	F	40	IA	EBC	Kanu
R_4	M	42	BA	OBC	Koeri
R_5	M	48	IA	OBC	Yadav
R_6	M	45	Matric	EBC	Kahar
R_7	F	42	8th Class	OBC	Koeri
R_8	M	48	IA	-	Muslim
R_9	M	45	BA	U. Caste	Rajput
R_{10}	M	50	IA	OBC	Yadav

All the ten respondent Panchayat Samiti members stated that Panchayat Samiti meeting is always presided over by the Pramukh and he keeps vigil at the officer at block level. Meeting of the Panchayat Samiti is convened every two months as stipulated. The Pramukh presents the annual financial statement before the Panchayat Samiti. They stated that the Panchayat Samiti meeting was never postponed for want of quorum. The first meeting of the Panchayat Samiti was presided over by the sub Divisional Magistrate in which the Pramukh and Deputy Pramukh were elected.

Only one of the seven respondents conceded that the Panchayat Samiti meeting was once disturbed and that it was one adjourned for want of quorum. Most of the members complained that the devolution of functions to the Panchayat Samiti is inadequate. It is less then what has been indicated in the Panchayat Raj Act. The State Government has not assigned functions in relation to matters to which the executive authority of the government extends. Members of the Panchayat Samiti averred that the General standing committee; finance, audit and planning committee; production committee; social justice committee; education committee; committee on public health, family welfare and rural sanitation, and public works committee have been constituted in the block. They stated that the Finance, Audit and Planning Committee has been discharging its functions.

However, they could not cite an instance when the Social Justice Committee would have performed or recommended to the Panchayat Samiti to perform any work related to social justice. They stated that no relief work has been undertaken in the block area through the Panchayat Samiti.

Panchayat Samiti members oversee rural housing and other public works construction activities in the block area. Though claiming that the Panchayat Samiti exercises its power to acquire, hold and dispose of property, members could not cite an instance of the Panchayat Samiti interning into contract or acquiring land for community development work.

With regard to the Panchayat Samiti Fund, the Members stated that it has not received any contribution and grant from the Zila Parishad or any other local authority. The Panchayat Samiti has neither received any loan from the state government nor it has raised on security of its assets. The Panchayat Samiti does not levy any toll, rates and fees. So its internal resource generation can be said to be nil. Panchayat Samiti has not earned from any construction and management work. The Panchayat Samiti has not received any gift or contribution. No trust or endowment has been made in its favour. The Panchayat Samiti has not imposed any fine or penalty luring the period.

As regards taxation, the respondent members stated that it has no tax income. It has not levied any fee on registration of vehicles or for providing sanitary arrangements. So far as the heat or market is concerned, collection of fees is done by the revenue department of the district administration.

As regards preparation of budget, members stated that it is done regularly and the attendance of members in such meetings being always more than fifty percent of the total strength. The Panchayat Samiti maintains its accounts that are properly audited. But members could not tell as to what action was taken by it on audit reports. Members told that the BPO acts as the executive officer of the Panchayat Samiti and he procures the cooperation of other staff members who have been appointed by the state government and received their salary from the government. The state government determines the service conditions of the staff of several departments posted of block level.

When the researches drew the attention of respondent Panchayat Samiti members towards the changes in the rural scenario, they struck a positive note. They stated that the general public consciousness has increased. They feel concerned for the solution of problems faced by them. They stated that elected women members at various tiers have functional autonomy. Members felt that the position/status of women has changed for the better.

The tried set of respondents was the members of the Gram Panchayat executive committee, popularly called word members. Altogether 33 word members were interviewed. Their replies to questions were almost the same on any issue. A separate questionnaire was prepared for them. They preferred to reply in terms of yet or no on any question. However, when quizzed further or encouraged to ventilate their experiences, some comments come that proved insightful for the investigation.

They concurred with respondent Mukhias that the meeting of Gram Sabha is organised regularly in each Gram Panchayat every three months with due notice to the village inhabitants. The office of the Gram Panchayat functions from the Panchayat Bhavan where a notice board is installed on which notice with regard to Gram Sabha meetings and all other relevant information is properly displayed. Members stated that the annual financial statement, budget, vigilance committee report, report of development programmes etc. are placed before the Gram Sabha. One being asked as to whether these reports are considered in the Gram Sabha meetings, they replied in affirmative. However, many of them conceded that most of the persons do not understand all the details. No instance of voting taking place in the Gram Sabha meeting could be cited by the respondent ward members, they stated that decisions in Gram Sabha meetings are always unanimous. Decisions are reached through consensus.

As regards quorum in Gram Sabha meetings, the respondent ward members stated that between 2001 to 2006, when rule was more stringent resolutions were mostly passed in the adjourned second meeting. The BPR Act 1993 section 5 (1) provided for one-tenth attendance. But in case meeting of the Gram Sabha has to be adjourned for want of quorum, the next meeting held next week on the some day and same time would require any mandatory attendance for quorum. The present BPR Act 2006 section 5 (1) provides for one-twentieth of the total members and in the adjourned next meeting it should be one-fortieth.

The respondent members stated that the attending villagers put their signatures in the proceeding book of the Gram Sabha during meeting. However, many a villagers complained that normally the register is kept at the residence of Mukhia and the public visiting Mukhia for any work have to sign it without looking into its contents. The respondent ward members told that sometimes the Block Development Officer or the Gram Panchayat supervisor visits during the Gram Sabha meetings. But such a situation seldom arises. In fact, when a meeting of Gram Sabha is arranged for specific purposes of the instance of the state government or a specific purpose camp or *Janta Darbar* is organised, the BDO or the GPS visits during the Gram Sabha meeting. Respondent ward Members stated that prior information of Gram Sabha meetings is always given to the Block Development Officer, Gram Panchayat Supervisor and the District Panchayat Raj Officer. Correspondents or representatives of newspapers at block level also come to know of Gram Sabha meetings.

Between 2001 and 2006, no meeting of Gram Sabha in any of the Gram Panchayats of Paroo block has to be convened by the executive officer. Such meetings are convened under Section 4(3) of the BPR Act when the Mukhia who is responsible for convening Gram Sabha meetings fails to do so any this fact is brought to the notice of the executive officer of the Panchayat Samiti (BDO). The respondent ward members stated that no complaint of non-convening of Gram Sabha meetings to higher authorities or to newspaper reporters has even been made in the Paroo block. So the question of any action being taken for non-convening does not arise at all.

Respondent ward members stated that vigilance committee has been constituted in their Gram Panchayats and its reports are placed in the Gram Sabha meetings. The executive officer of the Panchayat Samiti or any other government officer does not keep any eye on the placing of Gram Panchayat vigilance committee reports in the Gram Sabha meetings.

One of the important aspects of the working of Gram Panchayat is concerned with the relations between Mukhia and the members of Gram Panchayat (word members). A significant question arises as to whether the Mukhia takes the word members (Gram Panchayat Panchayat under section 12 of the BPR Act) into confidence while determining the priority of various developmental schemes. The respondent members stated that they are not always consulted. Schemes are passed by the Gram Sabha and the Mukhia has to execute only such schemes that receive sanction and fundings from the Zila Parishad. So, Mukhia performs prioritisation of programmes.

As regards their perception of apparent changes in rural scenario, the respondent ward members underlined that the social relationship among different communities has undergone change and accepted the new panchayat raj structure being one of its causational factors. Rural power structure has changed. The status of women in society has changed for the letter. The elected women members have acquired significant autonomy. They stated that mutual cooperation has increased of social level due to the working of the new Panchayati raj system.

From the general public, 100 respondents were selected from all the 34 Gram Panchayats. The sampling was done keeping in view the proportionate representation across gender, caste, sub caste, age group, economic class and educational attainment. Altogether 34 questions were put before then. Questions pertained to the Gram Sabha meetings, constitution of vigilance committee etc. Most of the replies were on similar lines. Meetings of Gram Sabha are regularly held after due notice including beating of drums. Office of the Gram Panchayat operates from the Panchayat Bhavan building. The BDO, Gram Panchayat Supervisor and the District Panchayat Raj Officer seldom visit during the Gram Sabha meetings. Signature of attending public is obtained on the register. Complaint of non-convening of Gram Sabha meetings are not normally lodged. Reports of the vigilance committee are placed before the Gram Sabha. People vouchsafe about perceptible change in rural scenario. Activities on various fronts are visible. They enumerate the construction of roads, bridges and culverts in rural area through the Panchayat Raj institutions. Schemes of water discharge, sanitation, and poverty alleviation have a positive impact. They underline that rural powr structure has changed, women has got opportunity to work in public realm in a big way. Their position has changed. They autonomously work.

Most of the respondent public say that rural society has earned harmony and cohesiveness through these institutions. The crumbling villages have been restored. Women have come out of the confines of four wall. However, a few discerning respondents from among the general public have different perception about the working of Gram Panchayats. Their replies to the 33 questions varied at several points. Notice about Gram Sabha meetings are given orally and only a few cohorts of Mukhia could know of the impending meeting in advance, says a college lecturer living in Saraiyya Panchayat of Paroo Block. He underlines that placing of statement of accounts, export of the preceding year, audit report and replies to it, annual budget for the forthcoming year, report about the development programmes undertaken and proposed and the report of the vigilance committee are not considered and deliberated upon in the Gram Sabha. These are only claimed to be placed before the Gram Sabha. He pointed out that Gram Sabha meets only on paper. Decisions are arrived neither unanimous nor by majority, but these are imposed by the Mukhiya. He says that officers responsible for ensuring regular meetings of Gram Sabha do not act upon the complaints of non-convening or flouting of norms. People are mostly unaware of the powers and functions of the vigilance committee at the Gram Panchayat level. Reports of vigilance committee are not read out and discussed in the Gram Sabha meeting, says the discerning respondent. The vigilance committee is packed of by the supporters of the Mukhia and it is the Mukhiya who gets the report prepared.

The BDO and other concerned officer do not keep vigil over placing of vigilance committee report in the Gram Sabha. This respondent is not optimistic about the role and position of elected women panchayat representatives.

Another respondent, who was Mukhia of Magurahian Panchayat between 2001 and 2006, was extensively interviewed by the researcher. He informed that no requisitioned meeting of Gram Panchayat executive committee was ever convened in any of the Gram Panchayats of Paroo block since 2001. the Panchayat Secretary, and sometimes the Gram Panchayat supervisor of block, attends the Gram Panchayat executive committee meeting. He concedes that meetings of Gram Sabha have to be adjourned several times for want of quorum. He also repeats what has been told by other Mukhia, word members, Panchayat Samiti member and Gram Sabha member respondents that the Gram Panchayat Officers function from the Panchayat Bhavan, vigilance committees have been constituted, Gram Sabha meetings are regularly organised after due notice and Gram Panchayats executive meet every two months. But he could not produce copies of Government orders related to devolution of funds, functions and functionaries. This respondent had been a schoolteacher before becoming Mukhia, but for him the distinction between devolution of functions to Gram Panchayats and the role of Gram Panchayats as implementing agencies of various government schemes was not clear.

He elaborated that the Gram Panchayat discharges only such functions as have been assigned to it by the government. It gets those schemes approved by the executive committee. He explicitly says that taxation power is not available to Gram Panchayats. When asked about year-wise allotment to Gram Panchayats on the recommendation of the State Finance Commission, he furnished the following information: 2001-2001 – Rs. 149364.00, 2002-2003 – Rs. 231355.00, 2003-2004 – Rs. 71281.00, 2004-2004 – Rs. 240567.00. He informed that accounts are properly maintained and audited. When asked about the Gram Raksha Dal and the appointment of its leader (Dalpati) he said that this provision was repealed through the BRP Act 1993.

Though he was, educated and served as Mukhia for five years, still unaware that through an amendment in 1995 (Bihar Panchayat Raj Amendment Act 1995, Act 14 of 1995) Section 32 A was inserted into the BPR Act 1993 that provided for organisation of Gram Raksha Dal. The BPR Act 2006 section 33 continues to have the same provisions. It reads as:

"For general watch and ward and for meeting emergent events like fire, flood, breach of embankment, collapse of bridge, outbreak of epidemic, to encounter burglary or dacoity etc or in order to perform such other duties that may be imposed by the government from time to time and for maintenance of public peace and order, a Gram Raksha Dal shall be organised under a Dalpati, appointed in the prescribed manner, for every Gram Panchayat and all bodies persons of a village between the ages of 18 and 30 years shall be members of the said Dal. The Government may makes rules for the organisation, duty and utilisation of Gram Raksha Dal."

It is clear that the government has not framed rules for the organisation duty and utilisation of the Gram Raksha Dal. The government has also not prescribed the rules and process in relation to the appointment of the Gram Raksha Dal. The respondent Mukhia (2001-2006) was oblivious of the provisions in the Act about the Gram Raksha Dal. It was not a solitary case.

The respondent Mukhia informed that most of the Mukhias are actively associated with self-help groups, cooperative societies and political parties. He said that due to the new Panchayati Raj Institutions, a spirit of cooperation, mutual dignity. Protection of public property, cordiality and desire to progress has enveloped the rural area. Development has acquired new meaning for the masses. Women have become articulate. They have become conscious of their role and responsibilities. They strive to work towards social enlistment.

Another important respondent was the Pramukh of Paroo block from 2001-2006. He was from the Scheduled Castes. He was interviewed on 25th January 2005 at the residence of the then member of Legislative Assembly who was a cabinet minister in the state government. The MLA has played crucial role in his election and sustained the Pramukh throughout his tenure at his continuous support. The Pramukh informed that he presides the Panchayat Samiti meetings that are held every two months. The meeting of Paroo Panchayat Samiti was never adjourned for want of quorum during his tenure. He cites instances of disruption during meeting over difference of opinion.

The response of Pramukh on presentation of annual financial statement before the Panchayat Samiti was in affirmative. Regarding launching of relief and rehabilitation measures, he informed that no such occasion ever arose during his tenure. He stated that rural housing, particularly Indira Awaas Yojana received his attention. He encouraged beneficiaries to complete their houses in time. He supervised entire gamut of activities mentioned in the Act. The Panchayat Samiti has not been assigned other works by the government, he said seeming oblivious of the existence of a slow of centrally sponsored schemes in which the Panchayat Samiti has to play major role in coordination.

All the standing committees of Panchayat Samiti have been constituted and are functioning well. The Pramukh of Panchayat Samiti appeared not aware of the powers regarding acquisition, holding and disposal of property and also of entering into agreement with other entities. Shops constructed on government land were allotted to the persons belonging to the scheduled castes, below poverty line, but the Panchayat Samiti has no role in it. Panchayat Samiti has no internal means of resource generation. It has neither levied any tax nor has it received any loan from the state government, Zila Parishad or other entities. No gift, donation or endowment has been received by the Panchayat Samiti.

The Pramukh, being aware of the fact that Panchayat Samiti can very tax, says that this power was never invoked considering impractical. Annual budget passed in the meeting of Panchayat Samiti becomes meaningless, as it has to depend on allocation by the state government for executing various schemes. As regards accounts and audit, the Pramukh stated that accounts are properly maintained and audited by auditors sent by the government. Employees are appointed and paid by the state government.

The Pramukh reported that he could not receive desired cooperation from the government employees as majority of them harbowe anti-scheduled caste feeling. This feeling hampers supervision of block work by him. However, he did not experience any interference by outside elements and reiterates that dalit and women representatives freely take decisions. They do not face external pressure. Dalits have socially gained. They take keen interest in resolution of problems faced by them.

The Pramukh desires that allocation of funds to Panchayat Raj Institutions by the state and central governments should be in accordance with the budgets passed by these bodies. The release of funds should be in one or two instalments between May and December every year to ensure timely utilisation. Release of grants in the next financial year should not depend on submission of utilisation certificate and completion of schemes of the preceding year. Delay in release of funds in accordance with budget mars the functioning of PRIs.

When the same questionnaire, that was given to Pramukh, was put before the *Block Development Officer* his answer to various questions were concise but differed on several significant points. The BDO clarified that the functions assigned to the Panchayat Samiti are not absolute. It has to wait for instructions from the district. Barring flood relief, no other specific work was assigned by the government. Paroo block was not affected by flood during the period. The BDO stated that accounts were always audited and no case of audit objection surfaced so far. The BDO stated that government directive to levy tax has not been received. The Panchayat Samiti prepares its budget but has to depend on government sanction and finance.

The BDO enumerates the following achievements achieved by the new Panchayat raj Structure : construction of village roads, digging of drinking water tubewells, construction of toilets, bridges, school buildings and panchayat bhavans. He accepts that rural power structure has changed, but women have to be educated to properly understand politics, administration, powers and functions of PRIs. He accepts that condition of women has considerably improved. He informed that no specific proposal for scheduled caste women has been chalked. Members of Panchayat Samiti never raised accountability and transparency questions during meetings. They have never tabled motions against employees for dereliction of duty, corrupt action, irregularity etc. But he accepts that completion has become endemic. It is very difficult to be immune from this disease.

Another set of respondents was secretaries of Gram Panchayats. Five secretaries were selected for operationalisation of questionnaires. All the five were male aged between 45 and 55. Three of them were matriculates and two were educated up to Intermediate Arts standard. Two of them were from other backward castes, while two belonged to upper caste Rajput. One of the Panchayat Secretary respondent was from Schedule Caste Paswan community. Among the two OBC respondents, one belonged to Annexure II Sah community while the other was an extremely backward caste Sahni.

All the five Panchayat Secretary respondents reported that Gram Sabha is regularly convened in their Gram Panchayats and the Gram Panchayat office is located in the Panchayat Bhavan. Vigilance Committee has been constituted in their Gram Panchayats. They said that notice regarding Gram Sabha is announced through dugdugi as well as pasting on the notice board of the Panchayat Bhavan. Four respondents reported that meeting of Gram Panchayat executive is convened every two months in their Gram Panchayats, while one respondent declined to answer this question. The situation to convene requisitioned meeting of Gram Panchayat executive on the call of one-third ward members has never arisen in the Gram Panchayats served by these secretaries.

The respondent ward members admitted that the meeting of Gram Sabha has to be adjourned several times for want of quorum, but the resolutions are passed in the reconvened meeting held after a week. The respondent ward members informed that the situation of Gram Sabha or Gram Panchayat meeting being presided by some other person in place of Mukhia as provided under section 21(4) has never arisen in their Gram Panchayats.

Questions were also asked about the functions of the Gram Panchayat. Asked about the functions developed to the Gram Panchayats, they said that functions of GPs are determined by the state government. They failed to produce photocopies of government letters. They admitted that GPs have not performed all the functions listed in the section 23 of the BPR Act. They stated that standing committees have been constituted under section 25. They have shown awareness about provisions of GP assets and funds under section 26. they admitted that in order to general internal resources, powers to impose taxes have been given to GPs under section 27 of the BPR Act. But, they stated that these powers could not be invoked, as it would have led to various practical difficulties. The respondent panchayat secretaries were reluctant to share information about the annual receipt of grants in each financial year since 2001. Similarly they did not show the copy of the annual budget of the Gram Panchayat since 2001. They also declined to show the proceeding books of the Gram Panchayat executive and Gram Sabha meetings.

The respondent Panchayat secretaries stressed that audit of Gram Panchayat accounts has been regularly done, but declined to show the audit reports.

Panchayat Secretaries are transferred by the District Magistrate. As regards the awareness about the powers and duties of the Panchayat Secretaries; they stated that Mukhia, UP Mukhia and ward members are aware, while most of the ordinary public are unaware. They reported that Gram Raksha Dal is not constituted in their Gram Panchayats. And the Dalpati is also not appointed. They reported that barring panchayat secretaries, no other functionary attends Gram Panchayat executive and Gram Sabha meetings.

It is interesting to note that all the five respondent

Panchayat Secretaries failed to enumerate the functions of the Gram Sabha, Gram Panchayat and the Mukhia. They stated that all the functions of Gram Sabha, Gram Panchayat are exercised by the orders of the Mukhia. They consider Mukhia to be the role executive decision maker of the Gram Panchayat.

When asked about the changes witnessed due to the new Panchayat Raj structure, they said that more attention has been given to roads, drinking water, school buildings etc. They underlined that rural power structure has changed but admitted that women elected representatives are yet to acquire full freedom from family control.

The researcher's probe into the devolution of funds, functions and functionaries through observation method threw the following data in relation to the Gram Panchayat and Panchayat Samiti. The observation focussed on the changes effected since 2006. the visit was held on 16th August 2008.

The functions of Gram Panchayat emanate from Article 243 G and the Eleventh Schedule of the constitution section 22 of the Bihar Panchayat Raj Act 2006 enlists 31 functions, while section 23 deals with the assignment of functions by the state government. Out of 31 heads mentioned in the section 22 the first is general functions. State government through its letter no-065 dated 17th June 2006 asked the Gram Panchayats to prepare annual plan for the development of the Panchayat area. It was fund during field observation that Gram Panchayats have prepared their annual plans. They have also prepared their annual budget. Gram Panchayats of Paroo Block have neither exercised their powers to take up relief works during natural calamities nor removed encroachment on public properties. No instance of organising voluntary labour came from any of the Gram Panchayats of Paroo block. So far as maintenance of essential statistic of villages is concerned, it was reported that the statistics was updated.

As regards other functions of the Gram Panchayats it was found that Gram Panchayats always look to the state government for specific orders. The functionaries of Gram Panchayats do not consider discussions held in meetings convened at block level as specific clear government instruction. So it was found that these Gram Panchayats have not taken any step for development of waste lands and maintenance of grazing lands including prevention of grazing lands' unauthorised – alienation and use. In fact, very few Gram Panchayats have earmarked grazing lands. Regarding agriculture, animal husbandary etc., the government orders of 2001 were to be applied. However, Gram Panchayats paid scant attention to them.

The state government directed Gram Panchayats to undertake land survey in their jurisdiction vide letter no-096 dated 19th July 2006. It was observed during field survey that Gram Panchayats have not taken up development of fisheries, planting and preservation of trees on the sides of roads and other public land under their control. Some steps towards promotion of from forestry and social forestry could be initiated during middle of 2009, when the divisional commissioner of Tirhut division took personal interest in the matter. However, its output and impact as also the role of Gram Panchayats in promoting these activities can be gauged only after a year.

It was observed the Gram Panchayats have taken no step as regards promotion of Khadi, village and cottage industries. Rural housing emerged as one of the foremost activity of Gram Panchayats. The state government instructed GPs to prepare Below Poverty Line (BPL) beneficiary list for prioritising the allocation of grants under Indira Awaas Yojana (IAY) vide leter no-215 dated 15th November 2006. Distribution of house sites, maintenance of records relating to house sites and other private and public properties remained in the hands of the circle officer, circle inspector and halka karmachari working under the control of the revenue department. The Gram Panchayats do not have control over these revenue functionaries.

As regards drinking water, a separate mission colled Prakalp undertakes these works with the assistance of several non-government organisations (NGOs). Tube wells have been repaired by the Gram Panchayats. MLAs also have a role in distribution of tube wells for drinking water, thus diminishing the role of the Gram Panchayats. Similar is the case with roads, culverts and bridges. Gram Panchayats have undertaken repair and strengthening of rural roads with the funds made available under tenth finance commission recommendations. The Gram Panchayats have also started various schemes of culvert and bridge construction for which instructions were issued by the Government vide letter no-317 dated 18th December 2006.

Regarding poverty alleviation programmes, it was observed that beneficiaries are formally selected in the Gram Sabha meetings. The GPs prepare panel for appointment for Panchayat Shikshas under the general control of education department officers vide letter no-1107 dated 7th December 2006. The state government has framed rules. The Gram Panchayats have convened meetings in their jurisdiction to ensure full enrolment and attendance in primary schools. The Gram Panchayats have started playing active role women and child development schemes. The state government has empowered Gram Panchayats vide letter no-7188 dated 26th July 2006 to select sites for Anganwadi Kendra and appoint Sevika and Sahayika for these centres. Panchayats were also empowered to monotor old-age and widows pension schemes vide letter no-1017 dated 21st February 2007. The Gram Panchayats of Paroo block have undertaken survey to select beneficiaries for the above schemes.

Through letter no-1/pp-1107 issued in 2007, the Gram Panchayats were assigned role in women's and child development activities, while letter no-SC/ Misc/3721 issued by the welfare department these Gram Panchayats were given role in implementation of the specific programmes for the welfare of weaker sections. It was observed that GPs have performed these roles. However, complaints were also received. The Gram Panchayats monitor the public distribution system, but these Gram Panchayats have no direct control over appointment suspension or cancellation of these PDS shops. The allotment of food grains, kerosene oil and other items is done by the civil supplies department under the control of the DM.

During field survey Mukhia of Bajitpur Gram Panchayat (Sanjiv Kumar) was extensively interviewed on devolution of functions on 16th June 2008. He has richly contributed in understanding this aspect of the present study.

Similarly a Panchayat Samiti women member elected from Magurahian Gram Panchayat area was extensively interviewed on 17th August 2008. The interview largely veered round the actual functions being performed by the Panchayat Samiti (the intermediate tier). The Panchayat Samiti also looked to the state government for specific instructions and have not undertaken all the functions mentioned in section 47 of the Bihar Panchayat Raj Act. The Panchayat Samiti was asked by the state government by letter no-080 dated 28th July 2006 to prepare annual plan and submit it to the Zila Parishad. It was also asked to consider and consolidate annual plan of all Gram Panchayats within the Panchayat Samiti and also to prepare annual budget. This task was performed annually.

Training of farmers and extension activities figures in S.47(2)(vi) as the function of Panchayat Samiti; but when agriculture fair was organised in the block premises in April 2008 the Panchayat Samiti members perceived it as being organised by the agriculture department not as a Panchayat Samiti function. Elected members consider only those functions as their functions in which they have to sign proceeding register or minute book or the Panchayat Samiti receive funds for the purpose that is spent through them This observation was found worth noting by the researcher. As in similar case it was found that the Panchayat Samiti met to consider government letter no-091 dated 12th April 2008 regarding poverty alleviation and upliftment of weaker sections. The matter was discussed, but the members felt that for want for clear instructions and funds at their disposal, nothing could be done. Panchayat Samiti members felt that no step was taken with regard to promotion of khadi, village and rural industries, as there was neither any specific direction nor any fund available for the purpose. Regarding Indira Awaas Yojana beneficiary selection, they feel that they have to approve the lists submitted by the Gram Panchayats. The IAY grants are made available by the state government.

It was observed that elected Panchayat Samiti members consider only when allocation of funds and directive to implement centrally sponsored schemes is received. Through letter no-218 dated 2nd September 2007, the Panchayat Samiti was asked to undertake road repair work under NREGS, it was acknowledged by members.

The state government has issued letters pertaining to every department in 2001, but since fund was not made available members do not consider these as their functions. State government's letter no-1097 dated 18th November 2006 was with regard to selection of Prakhand Shikshak. This task was performed adhering to the norms prescribed by the government. Construction, repair and maintenance of primary school buildings was done through Bihar Education Project (BEP) receiving funds from Sarva Shiksha Abhiyan (SSA). Panchayat Samiti members were found aware of their role in women's and child development (ICDS) schemes and mid-day meal scheme. Panchayat Samiti members perceived that having no control over allocation and lifting of materials meant for PDS shops and also no control over allotment, suspension and cancellation of shops meant that their mere monitoring power is of no consequence.

One of the articulate Panchayat Samiti member felt that the role of the intermediate tier has got reduced in post – 2006 phase as Gram Panchayats received added responsibilities. Panchayat Samitis have received funds only in relation to the National Rural Employment Guarantee Scheme that are spent on contruction and repair of rural roads, earth filling and brick soling, culvert construction etc. The matter of generating internal resources through tax imposition as envisaged in the Bihar Panchayat Raj Act 2006 has not come up for discussion in the Panchayat Samiti meetings. Income received from land revenue, settlement of *Sairaat*, markets, *haats* and fairs are deposited in the government accounts over which the Panchayat Samiti has no control.

Members felt that generation of internal resources through tax imposition is not feasible, Grants received out of the Tenth and the Eleventh Finance Commissions recommendations were cited as the only source of funds by many members of the Panchayat Samiti interviewed during field survey.

The hiatus between elected functionaries and the bureaucracy over which they have no control is reflected in a meeting that the Pramukhs have on August 25, 2008 at Patna. The Chief Minister of Bihar, Nitish Kumar, suggested to the Pramukhs of Panchayat Samitis to even go for sting operations to capture the panchayat department officials' illegal activities on camera. He said, 'several methods and modem gadgets and gizmos have been developed which are used these days to collect evidence against the wrong-doers.' Almost all panchayat pramukhs blamed the Block Development Officers for day to day interference in the Panchayats' functions. Pramukhs complained, "the BDOs say we have no power."

The Women Pramukhs accused the BDOs of not giving them due importance. One of the pramukhs from Kaimure district reportedly said before the Chief Minister, "Even my husband does not abuse me as much as the BDO does." Another Women Pramukh (Shamshad Khaton) from Katihar said that the BDO ignores them saying they are not MPs or MLAs. The BDO does not hold meetings of the Samiti – She Said, "when I go to this office, he does not offer me a chair to sit."[1]

In course of investigations data analysis and writing of the research report, the necessity to undertake latest field study and collect more relavant field data pertaining to working of Panchayati Raj Institutions in Paroo block was realised. Thus between 22 and 25 June 2009 filled visits were made. More data were collected as role of PRIs with respect to 17 aspects of working: -

(i) National Rural Employment Guarantee Scheme;

(ii) Other schemes out of the Twelfth Finance Commission Grants;

(iii) Indira Awaas Yojana;

(iv) Utilisation of Backward Region Grant Fund;

(v) Agricultural Development;

(vi) Health care sanitation etc;

(vii) Anganwadi Programme;

(viii) Education;

(ix) Aam Admi Bima Yojana;

(x) Old Age Pension Scheme;

(xi) Tax collection and resource generation;

(xii) Other funds;

(xiii) Scholarship to Scheduled caste students;

(xiv) Public Distribution System;

(xv) Allowances to the elected representatives;

(xvi) Role of the Pramukh at the block level; and

(xvii) Panchayat Fund.

NERGS

Each Gram Panchayat has a Rojgar Sevak to look after schemes under National Rural Employment Guarantee Act, who works under the supervision of the Programme Officer posted in every block. These functionaries are recruited by the government machinery, not PRIs. Schemes and work plons are prepared/approved by the Gram Panchayats and executed after approval from the Zila Parishad. Estimates are made by the Junior Engineer who does the measurement and certifies the works done. Flow of fund from the district is routed through the block level Programme Officer, BDO and Gram Panchayat Secretary do not have any role. Work under the scheme is assigned to job card holders who are paid at the rate fixed by the government. Wage is paid through post office saving account. Role of postal department becomes crucial in the execution of NREGs.

Though the elected representative do not have direct role, the quantum of allotment to a Gram Panchayat under the scheme depends, up to a great extent, on the efficiency of the Rojagar Sevak and the interest shown by the local representatives. For illustration, the figure[2] form Chochaihn Chapra Gram Panchayat for three financial years 2006-2007 (Rs. 1,55,000.00), 2007-2008 (Rs. 3,48,000.00) and 2008-2009 (Rs. 1,28,000.00) may be seen. It has been gathered from the block office that Gram Panchayats have spent varying amount under the scheme.

Twelfth Finance Commission

Under this head, funds are utilised for earth filling on road, providing drinking water facility and repair of houses. Paroo block received two instalments of Rs. 5993064.00 and

Rs. 5896750.00 in 2006-2007, two instalments of Rs. 6002428.00 each in 2007-2008 and two instalments of Rs. 6005725.00 in 2008-2009. Figures from a Gram Panchayat is indicative: Chochaihn Chapra received two instalments of Rs. 176296.00 each in 2006-2007, Rs. 176542.00 in 2007-2008 and two instalments of Rs. 176542.00 each in 2008-2009.

Every Gram Panchayats were also given Rs. 7500.00 each under Kabir cremation scheme during 2007-2008.

Schemes under Twelfth Finance Commission allocation are as usual prepared by Gram Panchayats and approved by the Gram Sabha. These are executed by the Mukhia and Panchayat Secretary. These are untied funds. Solar lights have also been provided under the scheme in addition to those mentioned in the beginning.

Indira Awaas Yojna (IAY)

The selection process of beneficiaries, quantum of grant and fund release process under IAY underevent significant changes in recent years. Earlier selection was made by the Mukhia who used to complete the formality of its passage by the Gram Sabha. From 2001-2002 to 2007-2008, Gram Panchayats prepared beneficiaries priority list and Panchayat secretaries used to supervise the house construction. Grants were revised from Rs. 20,000.00 to Rs. 24,000.00 in 2007-2008 and to Rs. 35,000.00 in 2008-2009. From 2008-2009, the beneficiaries are selected from the Panchayat / ward wise BPL priority list maintained at the district level and the amount is credited directly to his bank account in two instalments of Rs. 24,000.00 and Rs. 11,000.00 respectively. The second instalment is released after two months. They can withdraw the amount at this convenience.

During the field study in June 2009 it was found that many beneficiaries do not spend the amount in house constructions, instead they waste it is merry making. Mukhias and Panchayat Secretaries are lamenting the taking among of their control over selection, release of fund and house construction. However, the change in procedure by the government may be attributed to alarmingly large-scale complaint about extorting money from beneficiaries by the Mukhias, Panchayat Secretaries and the BDO during previous years. Loss of control by elected and other PRI functionaries seems justified, now even if money is being misused cases of bribery and commission charging in IAY selection and fund release have surely declined if not disappeared.

Backward Regions Grants Fund (BRGF)

BRGF has replaced the Rashtriya Sam Vikas Yojana. It is a centrally sponsored fund scheme operated through ministry of panchayat raj. Annual and Perspective Plan have to be prepared by each Gram Panchayat. It has wide spectrum of activities covering socio-economic and demographic information, agriculture and horticulture, livestock, infrastructure, drinking water and sanitation, road connectivity, flood proneness, self help groups, electrification, rural and cottage industries, other poverty alleviation schemes, economic sources of Gram Panchayat etc.

Schemes are prepared by the Mukhiya and passed by the Gram Panchayat executive and the Gram Sabha. The executive agency remains the Panchayat Secretary, who entrusts the work, though informally, to the confidants of the Mukhia. The BDO and the Junior Engineer are also concerned with administrative, financial and technical aspects of BRGF schemes. Complaints of misuse are widespread as there is no upper limit on the allocation. A Gram Panchayat can propose schemes of amount of million of Rupees. A Gram Panchayat of Katra block Changel has spent 62 lakh in previous year on dubious scheme about which even vigilance enquiry was initiated.

Agriculture etc

Agricultural fair is organised every year at block headquarters, in 2009 it was organised in June. Farmers can purchase farming implements, fartilisers, seeds etc. Improved paddy seeds were given to them. Block Agriculture officer and village level workers provide guidance and assistance to farmers. However, in Paroo block there are only six VLWs and 20 Panchayat Secretaries, so many VLWs are performing the duties of Panchayat Secretaries.

Health

Employees of State Health Department take care of health centres. ASHAs have been appointed in villages who receive instructions from the incharge of the block level primary health centre. Elected representatives have very little role in it.

Other Activities

No industrial, commercial and transportational establishment have come up at block level or in Gram Panchayats through the initiative of Panchayati Raj Institutions. Several centrally sponsored skill development, activities are running through non-government organisations and self help groups in which elected Panchayat Raj functionaries have played no role.

Education

Elected representatives have a role in appointment, inspection, salary payment and transfer of teachers. The number of vacancies in primary and middle schools are communicated by the block resource centre through Panchayat Secretaries. Appointment on contract basis through open advertisement based on merit following the reservation roster is made by Gram Panchayats and the Panchayat Samiti. These bodies adhere to the rules framed by the state government for the purpose. School education committee constituted at local level keep vigil over primary and middle schools teaching and development works.

Salary payment to teachers appointed by the PRIs are made from the funds received from Bihar Education Project (Sarva Shiksha Abhiyan). Cheques are signed jointly by the Mukhia and the Panchayat Secretary. Presently the procedure of bank advice and disbursement through teachers' bank account has been adopted. Gram Panchayats have to submit utilisation certificate to the BEP office. Transfer of teachers are made by a committee of Panchayat Samiti/Gram Panchayats in which secretary is also a member. Teahcers have to submit their casual leave application to the Panchayat Secretary.

Women and Child Development

The appointment of Anganwadi Sevika and Sahaika is made by the Child Development Project Officer on the basis of consensus arrived at Gram Sabha/Ward Sabha meeting. Mukhia, Panchayat Secretary, Ward members and the CDPO have decisive role in these selections. Salary of Sevika and Sahaika is paid out of child development project fund Mukhia inspects these centres. Panchayat Secretary does not have any role in relation to ASHA workers and Anganwadi centres, it was reported by a Panchayat Secretary in an interview conducted on June 22, 2009.

Social Security Schemes

Gram Panchayats are implementing a scheme called Aam Aadmi Bima Yojana in which state and control governments contribute the premium amount. Any resident aged between 18-60 is eligible it his total land possession does not exceed 0.50 acres. In case of accidental death an amount of Rs. 75,000.00 and natural death an amount of Rs. 30,000.00 is given to the insured person's dependents. In case of grievous injury during accident the surviving insured person is Rs. 37,500.00. The elected representatives have a role in propagating the scheme, while the Mukhia certifies his economic status on the basis of land records. The

Panchayat Secretary certifies his age.

There are two pension schemes: Indira Gandhi Old Age Pension Scheme and Laxmi Bai Social Security Pension Scheme for which beneficiaries are selected by the Gram Panchayats. Old age pension scheme meant for BPL cardholders has been extended to all needy persons aged above sixty five, an amount of Two hundred rupees is credited every month in the bank account of the beneficiary. The Panchayat Secretary has turn roles in it, first certifying the beneficiary and sending the bank advice. The Laxmi bai pension scheme is meant for destitute, disabled, widow person aged between eighteen and sixty-five. The beneficiaries are paid an amount of two hundred rupees every month through bank account.

Scholarship to Scheduled Caste Students

The scholarship amount is disbursed among the students from the scheduled castes families on the recommendation of school headmasters for which grant is received from the welfare department. The Panchayat Secretary sends the bank advice. Elected representative have no direct role in it.

Public Distribution System

Selection of beneficiaries of Annapurna, Antyodaya and BPL categories are made by the Gram Sabha. However, elected representatives do not have direct control over PDS shops. The upliftment is supervised by the supply officer posted at block level shops are sanctioned by the SDO/DM on the advice of ADSO/DSO.

Allowances to elected representatives

The state government has sanctioned allowances to the elected functionaries of the Panchayat Raj Institutions through its resolution no-2P/Vi 6-73/2006/PR/3011 dated 19th June, 2008 that was later modified by the resolution no-2P/

Vi 6-73/2006/PR/6159 dated 4th December, 2008. It was published in the extraordinary issue of Bihar Gazettee on 2nd January 2009. The following Table indicate monthly fixed allowance, daily allowance and travelling allowance of PRI elected representatives.

Table

Sl. No	*Designation*	*Fixed Monthly Allowance*	*Daily Allowance*	*Travelling Allowance*
1.	Chairperson, ZP	4000.00	100.00	5/- Per KM
2.	Vice Chairperson, ZP	3000.00	100.00	5/- Per KM
3.	Pramukh, PS	3000.00	100.00	5/- Per KM
4.	Up-Pramukh, PS	1500.00	100.00	5/- Per KM
5.	Mukhia, GP	600.00	100.00	5/- Per KM
6.	Up Mukhia GP	300.00	100.00	5/- Per KM
7.	Sarpanch, GK	600.00	100.00	5/- Per KM
8.	Up-Sarpanch, GK	600.00	100.00	5/- Per KM
9.	Member, ZP	-	100.00	5/- Per KM
10.	Member, PS	-	100.00	5/- Per KM
11.	Member, GP	-	100.00	5/- Per KM
12.	Member, GK (Panch)	-	100.00	5/- Per KM

In addition to the above allowances payable at uniform rate, the representatives of both sexes male and female from the scheduled castes, scheduled tribes and extremely backward castes and female representatives from other social categories who are living below the poverty line are paid a special honorarium at the rate of rupees one hundred per meeting. For the travelling allowance the distance is calculated from the residence as mentioned in the nomination paper, of the elected member and the headquarters of the concerned PRIs. Daily allowance and travelling allowance is admissible for attending the general/special/standing committee meeting of the PRIs and sitting of the Gram Panchayat Katchary bench.

These allowances are being paid with effect from April 1, 2008.

Untied Funds

Enquiries in relation to untied funds available to Panchayats reveal that Mukhia of a Gram Panchayat has no such fund at his disposal. None of the Gram Panchayats of Paroo block have undertaken any work out of untied fund.

The open ended interviews conducted with seven Panchayat Secretaries, at block headquarters in June 2009 brought to fore several aspects of the working of PRIs. It was gathered that elected representatives are always apprehensive change in reservation roster of their seats. They do not pay as much attention to their wards, panchayats or territorial constituencies as was given by the representatives prior to 2006. They felt that their unreserved seat may become reserved for any other category next time or any unreserved seat may also become unreserved or reserved for other categories. However, the sate government in late 2009 declared its intention to half delimitation for one more term. This decision of the government is expected to bring about attitudinal change in elected representatives who have thought that they would not have to the electorate next time for votes and become negligient towards their electorate.

The impact of reservation in PRIs has transformed the rural social life generating aspirations among various segments to become representative in future. This tendency has energised rural political scene growing leadership ambitions. Change from 1978 and 2001 scenarios is manifest. Change in social composition of elected representative and presence of large number of elected women representatives have changed the rural life. Sizeable presence from the scheduled castes and the extremely backward castes has transformed the rural power structure. People have high hopes from these institutions.

As regards the appraisal of the working of the Panchayat Samiti is concerned, its role has been reduced to a great extent. Now Gram Panchayats receive BRGF funds, different Finance Commission Funds, NREGS funds, other district and state plan funds and funds meant for centrally or state sponsored schemes directly. The amount is either straight way credited to Gram Panchayat accounts or cheques are issued by the district authorities to the Gram Panchayats. The formality of Gram Sabha meeting is being altered, however Gram Panchayats complain of inadequate fund remains. Gram Panchayats can accord administrative approval for schemes upto Rupees one lakh, while it has to obtain approval from block for expenditure on schemes with higher estimated amount. Panchayat Samiti or BDO do not disburse any amount to Gram Panchayats directly get fund from Zila Parishad, Panchayat Samiti merely consolidates the schemes prepared by Gram Sabha that is construed as recommendation. Panchayat Samiti or BDO, however, receives monthly reports from Gram Panchayats and forwards it upwards. Loss of direct control over disbursement of funds to Gram Panchayats has weakened the position of the Panchayat Samiti members vis-à-vis Gram Panchayats.

So, far as the office of the Pramukh is concerned, the data gathered from Paroo reveal certain significant facts. The office is reserved for extremely backward caste women. A Muslim EBC candidate Meharunissa was elected to the post in whose election the MLA of Sahebganj constituency played to decisive role. Majority of Paroo block Gram Panchayats tell in that assembly constituency while Paroo assembly constituency comprised of Saraiya block Gram Panchayats and rest of Paroo Gram Panchayats. The MLA blongs to the ruling Janta Dal (United) party and Paroo MLA belongs to the Bartiya Janta Party. Both of them belongs to the some upper caste and support the ruling

National Democratic Alliance coalition state government. Most of the Paroo block Panchayat Samiti members belong to JDU and the Sahebganj MLA has enormous influence over them. The opposition Rashtriya Janta Dal has few supports among the elected Panchayat Samiti members.

Since the office of the Pramukh is reserved for extremely backward caste woman, other members of the Panchayat Samiti have least interest in factional polities even if they are dissatisfied. Another facts in the feat of inviting the wroth of the MLA, reported many respondents. In 2008 a no confidence motion was tabled that received only votes. The Pramukh being a non-controversial and courteous person is also a reason of least opposition faced by her. Panchayat Samiti meetings are normally smooth and cordial. Most of the members are themselves involved in the execution of NREGS schemes and do not want to raise issues. Another factor contributing to the strength of the Pramukh is frequent transfer of the Block Development Officer of Paroo.

One important revelations that came was related to the execution of NERGS. Panchayat has to be made to the accounts of the job cardholders and the Rojgar Sevak is the formal implementation agency. In fact the scheme is executed by the Panchayat Samiti members who has to pay the wage in cash to the labourers who have worked at the site. He merely uses the job card number of the cardholders in preparing muster rolls. Field experiences suggest that job cardholders may have migrated or may be unwilling to work but lend their card number for use. They have to draw amount from their account and give it to the *theekedar* for disbursement in cash to actual workers. The Gram Panchayats do not have direct role in it, Rojgar Sevak acts under programme officer's guidance. There exists ample scope of pilferage of funds under this informal procedure. It has increased corruption is rural areas. Sometimes quarrel between job cardholders whose card number has been used and *Theekdar* erupt creating enmity and police case in which the actual reason of fight is not revealed. Programme Officers, Junior Engineer and Rojgar Sevak is collusion with the *Theekdar* representative siphon off the fund, it was reported during field investigation.

Another aspect is the women's political empowerment that has surely been achieved through representation ensured by fifty percent reservation. Women elected representatives having largely given up their inhibition are participating vigorously and largely getting their due in terms of social respectability and say in decision making. In field visit it has been learnt that a few scheduled caste and women representatives face difficulty in discharging their respeonsibilities. To cite a few concrete examples, reports about Jyoti Devi (SC) of Mohaffatpur, Rajdeo Ram (SC) of Baijalpur, Indradeo Ram (SC) of Rampur Kesho Malahi, Gita Devi (General) of Fatehabad and Anita Devi of Zafarpur Gram Panchayats have received that they depend on others' assistance.

Social audit is another significant aspect of the working of PRIs. Through social audit transparency and accountability of these institutions can be enhanced. Gram Sabha is an important instrument for this purpose. It may be hoped that in course of time its instrumentatility in real terms would increase. Self help groups have emerged as an instrument of enhanced mobilisation for economic upliftment. These community organisations have been mandated as essential part of Swaranjayanti Gram Swarojgar Yojana (SGSY), a centrally sponsored flagship scheme.

Panchayati Raj Institutions have not started playing role in electrification schemes, though in propagation of non-conventional energy sources, their role was found visible during field visits. Elected Panchayat functionaries have mentioned that PRIs have not been provide control over forests and water bodies, these are still with the forest and fishers departments respectively. These are government owned and continue to be so. They pleaded for transferring ownership to PRIs. Taking away of financial powers, particularly joint signature on cheques by Zila Parishad chairperson and Panchayat Samiti Pramukh was mentioned. Mukhias financial powers in relation to disbursement of Indira Awaas Yojana funds have also been curtailed. In NREGS matters, Mukhia signs cheques jointly with Rojgar Sevaks and in Panchayat teachers salary disbursement Mukhia signs cheques jointly with the Panchayat Secretary. The BDO has been entrusted with the task of approval of old age pensioners list. The autonomy of Mukhia inadministrative matters has reduced. District Magistrates have stopped attending Zila Parishad meetings so as the sub divisional officers in case of Panchayat Samitis. In Bihar, the Deputy Development Commissions have been replaced by the District Magistrates as the district programme coordinator of the NREGs scheme. Similarly the Rojgar Sevaks have been placed under the block level programme officers. Earlier they were placed under Mukhia. PRIs have emerged, in fact, as another extension of the field machinery of the state government.

Summing up the PRIs have travelled a lot since their inception. The 73rd Amendment could be implemented in Bihar only in 2001 that inromically in truncated from with no reservation for scheduled castes and women on chairperson solitary posts. Full throttled functioning with reservation provisions could come only in 2006. Devolution in incomplete as activity mapping is inconclusive. The Ministry of Panchayat Ram (MOPR) of the union government has lunched a scheme called Panchayat Empowerment and Accountability Incentive Scheme (PEAIs) that evoluates states on various scores and rewards the states performing well. Assessment for the year 2008-2009 was announced on 3rd March 2009 vide letter no-MOPR-N-11013/2/2006-Pol.II. Only states were evaluated that have qualified the framework criteria based on four fundamental constitutional requirements getting fulfilled. These requirements are holding of PRI elections, establishment of state finance commission and State Election Commission and also constitution of District Planning Committees.

Among the states evaluated that have qualified the above criteria, Bihar ranked at the 19th position based on three items devolution of functions, finances and functionaries. Its score in terms of functions (3.60) and functionaries (2.43) were satisfactory. But in terms of devolution of finances, its score was 0.73. It was so because PRIs in Bihar neither generate internal resources nor impose taxes.

Conclusively, in the present chapter an appraisal of the working of PRIs in Paroo was attempted. It has been modestly accomplished on the basis of empirical data collection and analysis. In the next chapter findings of the study would be exhaustingly presented.

5

Conclusion

India's march towards empowerment at the grassroots and rural development progressed through the politically representative and administratively devolved new Panchayat Raj institutions, which came into existence post 1973. The year 1993 proved to be a turning point in the evolution of local self governing institutions in India as they were provided constitutional status. The constitution (Seventy-Third) Amendment Act 1992 that came into force on 24th of April 1993 is considered a watershed development in the history of decentralised governance, planning and development. Local self government today is not at the mercy of state government concerned. From the position as an entry in the state List of the Schedule VII, it now stands as Part IX of the Constitution of India. Every detail of its structure and various functionaries have been provided in Articles 243 to 243 0. Schedule XI enlists the 29 functions to be performed by these institutions. In terms of power and authority, the Panchayat Raj Institutions have emerged as the third tier of government with reasonable substance and contents. This step created space for women and marginalised groups in the federal set-up of India.

The introduction of the new scheme was widely hailed as it sought to impart certainty continiuty and strength to the Panchayat Raj institutions. It did casts a duty on the union as well as on state governments to establish and nourish village panchayats as to make them effective, self governing institutions. The government claimed to have fulfilled Mahatma Gandhi's dream of gram swaraj.

The state of Bihar also moved in implementing the scheme, but the first elections could be held in the year 2001 and the second in 2006. The Reservation scheme, as envisaged in the legislation, for women and socially disadvantaged groups also underwent changes, due to judicial intervention and later political decision to widen it.

This study sought to decipher as to how far the expectations generated about the new scheme have been realised in Bihar. It sought to grasp the changes witnessed in rural social scenario as also in its power structure. The changes in type of leadership in terms of gender, caste, class, occupation and age was also considered as indicators in grasping the rural transformation. The question was that whether the reservation for women or their actual presence in the Panchayats have made any immediate impact. Regarding women elected representatives questions about the role of their family members in the PRI affairs and the respect shown to them were also pertinent. The status of devolution of functions, funds and functionaries were also significant.

Through the present study, an attempt was made to review the working of Bihar Panchayat Raj Act 1993 and 2006 through a case study of Paroo block Panchayat Samit and its 34 Gram Panchayats. It sought an examination of correlation between the formal powers and functions of PRI vis-a-vis the administrative, financial, functional and technical support that these bodies posses. It also sought to assess the impact of overlapping functions between two tiers n Gram Panhayats and Panchayat Samitis.

This study began with these hypotheses :-

1. Rural scenario of Bihar, particularly its power structure, witnessed major changes due to the new PRIs.
2. It new type of leadership in terms of caste, class, gender, age and occupation has come at the lower levels.
3. Despite being elected in fair number due to reservation, women and the Scheduled Castes are yet to acquire the actual leadership role and position.
4. Devolution of functions, funds and functionaries are not adequate.
5. Gram Sabhas are yet to become a genuine mode of participatory democracy.

In order to test these hypotheses, the research work was conducted empirically grounded in field work – observation and experience.

The date collection was done inter alia, through participant observation and unstructured interview. Though the work was intended to be diagnostic some exploration was also aimed at. Questionnaires were operationalised to the sampled elected representatives, government functionaries, and members of general public. Scanning of relevant government documents – Acts, Notifications, Byelows, Reports of the Parliamentary Standing Committee, Ministries of Rural Development and Panchayati Raj, Proceedings of the Union and state legislatives – as also of scholarly writings published in books, journals and newsreports and analyses were relied upon for inputs.

This study aimed to shed lights on the status of devolution, participation, accountability and transparency aspects of the PRIs in Bihar. It was found that PRIs in Bihar face three-fold challenges. First challenge is the tardy pace of devolution of functions, functionaries and finance. Discussion on devolution led the researcher to seek answer to the questions regarding (i) extent of devolution, (ii) impact of complex three-tier organically linked structure three tier structure that disregards the vital principle of subsidiarity on smooth functioning (iii) the nature and extent of control exercised by the PRIs over government servants at district and sub-district levels, and (iv) the nature and extent of de-facto and de-jure powers exercised by the PRIs.

The second challenge relates to participation. Participatory democracy at the local level can be institutionalised only when the Gram Sabha becomes functional in real terms. The researcher observed that to emerge as an instrument of direct participatory democracy at the gross-roots the Gram Sabhas have to really meet at three months as prescribed in Section 3 of the BPR Act 2006 and seriously deliberate the matters listed in section 7. The Gram Sabhas are to consider the annual statement of accounts of the Gram Panchayat, the annual report, audit note and its replies, the Gram Panchayat budget, vigilance committee reports and development programmes. The Gram Sabhas in Paroo block found to be wanting in these respects. These were only formally discharging these responsibilities and meeting the legal requirements. The law enables the Gram Panchayats to act for removal of encroachments on public properties and organise voluntary labour and contribute to community works. None of the Gram Panchayats of Paroo block were acting in these directions.

Accountability and transparency emerged as another dimension of challenge before PRIs in Bihar. The researcher found constraints in the path of ensuring these values. The level of integrity, autonomy and commitment to public interest of elected Panchayat functionaries was observed to be low. The Pramukh, chairperson of the Panchayat Samiti, was able to secure his position due to the influence of the local member to the legislative assembly.

The researcher sought to find ways to remove these weaknesses so that the Gram Panchayats and Panchayat Samities can function as vibrant, full-blooded, third tier of the federal set-up. The researcher finds that the optimism about decentralisation providing greater transparency, accountability, responsiveness, probity, frugality, efficiency, equity and opportunities for mass participation needs compatible social environment and political culture to produce results. However, the social environment and political culture are slow to change.

The new PRI scheme has, undoubtedly, secured political representation through reservation. Thus the empowerment of women, Dalits and other marginalised groups such as extremely backward castes in Bihar has been substantially achieved. But, at the some time, the PRIs have emerged as the field agencies of the central and state governments implementing programmes sponsored by the government in accordance with government guidelines. These programmes range from development to social security, job creation and poverty alleviation schemes.

Devolution involves 3Fs-functions, funds and functionaries. These three are complimentary to one another in the devolution of responsibilities and powers upon Panchayats. These seven elements constitute devolution. These are :-

(i) Allocation of functions

(ii) Allocation of funds

(iii) Provision of functionaries

(iv) Administrative control over staff

(v) Transfer of programmes and scheme along with budget and staff

(vi) Freedom to take administrative and financial decisions.

(vii) Capacity building measures.

The cardinal principle of subsidiarity on which devolution was to be based upon means that each tier has functions appropriate to that level. However, the activity mapping is yet to be completed in Bihar while other states have done so long ago.

So, it can be concluded that the objective of creating strong base of political empowerment of ordinary people has been largely achieved. But as the 73rd Constitutional Amendment mandates to give the PRIs a significant degree of autonomy and impart to them an element of self-reliance and self sufficiency through fiscal transfers, taxation powers and tax assignments. Yet, there is considerable ambiguity about the role the Panchayats have to play. These institutions appear to have been superimposed on the existing administrative hierarchy at the district level. The administrative frame consisting of the field establishments of the line departments of the state government and the offices under the control of the District collector such as the offices of the Deputy Development Commissioner/Sub Divisional Officer/Block Development Officer remains intact and continues handling all the regulatory, developmental and residual functions of the government as usual with the elected Panchayati Raj Institutions discharging minor roles in rural development schemes.

The requirement is that most of the functions/activities now being performed by the state government agencies at the local level have to be withdrawn from them and handed over to the panchayats together with functional autonomy and adequate resources in discharging those activities. But this has not happened and the tendency to look at Panchayats as another extension of the field machinery of the state government still persists.

To strengthen Panchayats as the third tier of government, following suggestions are being advanced.

First, functions and activities need to be identified that would be exclusive domain of the PRIs, and some areas of activities where the state government and Panchayats could work as equal partners with concurrent jurisdiction.

Secondly, the PRIs act as agencies of the state government for implementing some state schemes or centrally sponsored poverty alleviation and other schemes, but other activities are also required to enable the PRIs to emerge as the local government. A suitable balance needs to be worked out among these roles. Effective service delivery, fair distribution of the fruits of development, accountability and people's involvement in participatory planning could be made the goals of decentralisation.

Thirdly, the wording of Article 243 G leaves considerable leeway with the state government in the whole scheme of things.

Fourthly, the issue of decentralisation could be served better if the function are transferred by an act of legislative.

Fifthly, the issue of decentralisation would be served better if there is a third list of local functions in the 7th schedule itself along with the presently occurring Union, State and Concurrent Lists.

Sixthly, devolution of an activity should be accompanied by the placement of state government staff attached to the devolved activities to the appropriate tiers of the PRIs under the condition that they would remain fully responsible to and under the disciplinary control of elected authority.

Seventhly, elementary education, adult and non-formal education, primary health care, drinking water, sanitation, women and child development, civic services, roods and rural infrastructure including rural electrification should be exclusively assigned to Panchayats.

Eighthly, it is essential that the structural involvement of Panchayats is ensured in the implementation of Centrally Sponsored Schemes like Integrated Child Development Scheme and Sarva Shiksha Abhiyan, which have a tendency to prescribe formation of programmatic committees, which are out side the permanent structure of the local governments. These parallel committees for schools, health care etc. cause confusion and conflict at local level.

Various levels of Panchayats in Bihar are yet to acquire role clarity for want of incomplete activity mapping.

The study has been presented in five chapters.

The introductory first chapter begins with the discussion on the concept of decentralisation in democratic governance as it has evolved in India. It focuses on significant landmarks in the progress of Panchayati Raj System in India. With reference to Bihar it traces the institutional evolution which has been dealt with the field studies. This chapter has been done in four parts. The Part I deals with the concept, theoretical foundation, rationale of local self government as also the idea of Panchayats in Indian villages right from ancient times to the days of Gandhi. The Part II traces the important evolutionary landmarks of British period since the East India Company days. The Part III focuses on constitution making, while the Part IV dealt evolution thereafter covering the constitutional scheme, Community Development Programmes, Balwantrai Mehta, Ashoka Mehta and other committees' recommendations, and the attempts to provide the PRIs constitutional status during late 1980s and early 1990s. It also briefly covers the salient features of the 73rd CAA 1992 and the Bihar situation.

The second chapter dealt with the structural framework of the new Panchayati Raj System in Bihar covering the legislative enactments of 1993/95 and 2006 and several judicial pronouncements relevant to the study. The second chapter has also been done in four parts. The first part covered the structural framework including the composition, powers and functions of various offices and bodies. The second part dealt with the reservation provision and roster etc. The third part discussed inter-relationship between various organs, while the fourth part presented a concluding summary of the presently obtaining structural framework.

In the third chapter, the researcher sought to examine the status of devolution of functions, finance and functionaries.

The fourth chapter purported to present an appraisal of the working of the Panchayati Raj Institutions in the Paru block of Muzaffarpur district in Bihar. It was completely dependent on field-work based data collection for which reliance was placed on operationalisation of questionnaires and conducting unstructured open ended interviews.

So far as the findings of the study are the concerned, all the five hypotheses have been tested and found valid.

Bibliography

1. Primary Sources

A. Interview

B. Questionnaires

C. Election results of 1978, 2001 and 2006 for Panchayati Raj Institutions in Muzaffarpur District, Particularly Parool Block.

D. Detailed Informations as regards class, caste, gender, age and occupation of elected representative — Panchayat members and office bearers.

E. Proceedings of the meetings of Gram Sabhas Village Panchayat executives and the Panchayat Samiti.

F. Government Circulars, Notifications, Act, Bye laws, Reports and other relevant Documents

1. Constituent Assembly Debates accessed at the Website of Law Ministry, Government of India.
2. Constitution of India as amended up to date accessed at the website of Law Ministry, Government of India.
3. Bihar Gram Panchayat Act 1947.
4. Bihar Zila Parishad and Panchayat Samiti Act 1961.
5. Bihar Panchayat Raj Act 1993.

6. Bihar Panchayat Raj (Amendment) Act 1995, Bihar Act 14 of 1995.

7. Bihar Panchayat Raj (Amendment) Act 1996, Bihar Act 5 of 1996.

8. Bihar Panchayat Raj (Amendment) Act 2003, Bihar Act 17 of 2003.

9. बिहार पंचायत निर्वाचन नियमावली, 1995.

10. बिहार पंचायत निर्वाचन (संशोधन) नियमावली 2001

11. Bihar Panchayat Raj Ordinance 2006 (Ordinance no. 1 of 2006), to repeal and replace the Bihar Panchayat Raj Act, 1993 as amended upto date, Bihar Gazettee (Extraordinary) dated 14 January 2006.

12. Bihar Panchayat Raj Act 2006 (Bihar Act 6 of 2006).

13. Bihar Panchayat Raj (Amendment) Act 2006.

14. Bihar Panchayat Raj (Amendment) Act 2007.

15. Report of the V. Ramchandran led Expert Group, Planning at the Grassroots Level: An Action Programme for the Eleventh Five Year Plan, Ministry of Panchayati Raj, New Delhi, March 2006, pp. 1-91.

16. Study on Elected Women Representatives in Panchayati Raj Insttutions, Ministry of Panchayati Raj, Government of India, New Delhi, April 2008, pp. xiii + 161.

17. Mani Shankar Aiyar, Panchayati Raj in India: The Greatest Experiment in Democracy Ever, Ministry of Panchayati Raj, Government of India, New Delh, October 2006, pp. 1-123.

18. Report of the Task Force led by K. Saxena on Panchayati Raj Institutions, Planning Commission, New Delhi, December 2001, pp. 1-135.

19. Report of the Task Force on Devolution of Powers and Functions to Panchayati Raj Institutions led by Lalit Mathur, Panchayati Raj Division, Department of Rural Development,

Ministry of Rural Development, Government of India, New Delhi, 2002, pp. 1-104.

20. A Compendium of Resolutions of the Seven Round Tables of Ministers In-Charge of Panchayati Raj, July-December 2004, Ministry of Panchayati Raj, Government of India, New Delhi, June 2006, pp. 1-40.

21. Background Note and Action Points for Chief Minister's Conference on Poverty Alleviation and Rural Prosperity Through Panchayati Raj, Ministry of Panchayati Raj, 2007, pp. 1-15.

22. 37th Report on Implementation of Part IX of the Parliaments Standing Committee on Urban and Rural Development tabled in both House of the Parliament in November 2002.

23. Agenda Notes for the Meeting of the Empowered Sub-Committee of the National Development Council on Financial and Administrative Ministry of Panchayati Raj and Planning Commission, 12 June 2006, pp. 1-34.

24. State-Wise Status of Devolution to Panchayati Raj Institutions, Fact-Sheet: Bihar, PRIA, New Delhi, July 2004, pp. 21-43.

25. Annual Report 2005-06, Ministry of Panchayati Raj, Government of India, New Delhi, 2006.

26. Annual Report: 2006-2007, Ministry of Panchayati Raj, New Delhi, 2007.

27. Annual Report: 2007-2008, Ministry of Panchayati Raj, New Delhi, 2008.

28. Annual Report: 2008-2009, Ministry of Panchayati Raj, New Delhi, 2009.

29. Report of the Committee of Secretaries, Co-Chaired by Renuka Vishwanathan, Secretary (Coordination) Cabinet Secretariat and Meenakshi Datta Ghosh, Secretary, Ministry of Panchayati Raj, on 'Centrally spousored schemes : Identifying a domain for Panchayati Raj Institutions.

30. Conclusions of the Conference of academies on 'Inclusive Growth through Inclusive Governance : The Future Agenda for Local Government, organised by Ministry of Panchyayati Raj on 25 & 26 February 2009, pp. 1-10 (*http://www.panchayat.gov.in*).

31. Report of the Second Administrative Reforms Commission on Panchayati Raj, 2008.

32. An Index of Devolution for Accessing Environment for Panchayati Raj Institutions in the States, Empirical Assessment 2008, Final Report prepared by the National Council of Applied Economic Research (NCAER) for the Ministry of Panchayati Raj, March 2009, pp. iv+71.

33. Categorisation of Gram Panchayat Remands, Experiences; Examples, Consolidated Reply, Solution Exchange for the Decentralisation Community, UNDP, 115 April, 2009.

34. Consolidated Reply to the query from DFID, New Delhi on examples, Advice regarding Decentralisation Monitoring Indicators, UNDP Solution Exchange for the Decentralisation Community, 7 December 2005.

35. Consolidated Reply to the query 'Resources on Ranking Indian States in Terms of Devolution', Examples, Experience and Advice', UNDP Solution Exchange, 16 March 2009.

36. बिहार गजट, असाधारण अंक, पंचायती राज, विभाग, 2 जनवरी, 2009.

37. अधिसूचना 93, पंचायती राज विभाग, 19–1–2009.

38. Notification 4383, Panchayati Raj Department, 26.8.2008.

39. अधिसूचना 5890, पंचायती राज विभाग, 19–11–2008.

40. State of the Panchayat, 2007, State Profile: Bihar, Ministry of Panchayati Raj, 2008, pp. 1-13.

41. Committee on Plan Projects, Report of the Team of the study of Community Projects and National Extension Service, Vol. 1, New Delhi, 1957, p. 7.

42. Extract of High Court order as published in the Patna edition of the Times of India on July 5 and 6, 2000, p. 12, p. 5.

43. National Common Minimum Programme of the Unitied Progressive Alliance, New Delhi, 2004.

44. Patna High Court Order in CWJC No. 3351 of 1994, and analogous cases, Extract of the order was published in the Patna edition of the Times of India for five consecutive days from June 22 to 26 1996 at, p. 12, p. 6, p. 12, p. 12 and p. 12 respectively.

45. Report, Working Group on Decentralised Planning and PRIs, Planning Commission, November, 2001.

G. Newspapers & Periodicals

(1) Hindustan (Hindi)

(2) Hindustan Times (English)

(3) Dainik Jagran

(4) The Hindu

(5) Panchayati Raj Update

(6) Kurushestra.

2. Secondary Sources

A. Books

1. Agarwal Pramod Kumar, भारत में पंचायती राज, Gayan Ganga, 2005.

2. Arora Puranchand, बिहार राज्य पंचायत अधिनियम एवं बिहार पंचायत निर्वाचन नियमावली, Pahuja Law House, Pirmuhani, Patna-800003

3. Arora Puranchand, बिहार पंचायत राज अध्यादेश, 2006, और बिहार पंचायत निर्वाचन नियमावली, 2006, Pahuja Law House, Pirmuhani, Kadamkuwan, Patna-800003

4. Basu Durga Das, Introduction to the Constitution of India, Wadhwa and Company Law Publishers, New Delhi, 2006.

5. Basu Durga Das, Bharat Ki Samvaidhanic Vidhi, Prentice Hall of India, New Delhi-2001.

6. Biju M.R., Dynamics of New Panchayati Raj System: Reflections and Retrospections, Kanishka Publishers and Distributors, New Delhi,1998.

7. Cunningham, Frank, Theories of Democracy : A Critical Introduction, Routledge, London, 2002.

8. Chopra Saroj, स्थानीय प्रशासन, Novelty & Company, Patna, 1999.

10. Devady Kamala, Education Philosophy of Gandhi, Sri Publishing House, New Delhi, 1998.

11. Jain Pukhraj & Fadia B.L., 'भारतीय शासन और राजनीति, Sahitya Bhawan Publications, Agra, 2008.

12. De Mello L. R. and Kichiro Fukasaku, Fiscal Decentralisation in Emerging Economics Development Centre OECD, Paris, 1999.

13. Gandhi M.K., Hind Swaraj or Indian Home Rule, Revised New Edition Eight. Reprint- Navajeevan Publication House, Ahmedabad, 1990.

14 Jana, Anil Kumar, Adminstring District Plans in India, Concept Publishing Compnay, New Delhi, 2004.

15. Jha. S.N. and Mathur P.C., Decentralization and Local Politics, Sage Publications, New Delhi- (Thousand Okks London), 1999.

16. Jha Chatakar, Bhartiya Sthaniya Swashasan, Novely and Company, Patna, 2001.

17. Joshi R.P., Constitutionalization of Panchayat Raj, Concept Publishing Company, New Delhi.

18. Jha Chatakar, Local Government by Committee, Novelty and Company, Patna-4.

19. Laski, Harold J., A Grammer of Politics, S. Chand, Delhi, 1979.

20. Maheshwari S. R., Bhartiya Prashashan, Bhartiya Prashasan, Orient Lognman Pvt. Lt., New Delhi, 2004.

21. Malhotra V.K., Bihar Panchayat Raj Act 1993, Malhotra Brothers, Patna, 1994.

22. Maheshwari S. R., भारत में स्थानीय स्वशासन, Centre for Political and Adminstrative Studies, New Delhi, Lakshmi Narain Agarwal, Agra, 2003.

23. Maheshwari S.R., Local Government in India, Lakshmi Narayan Agarwal, Agra, 2004.

24. Manor James and Crook, C. Richard, Democracy and Decentralization in South Asia and West Africa, Cambridge University Press, 1998.

25. Mahipal, Gap Between Needs and Resources of Panchayats in India, Mittal Publication, New Delhi, 2003.

26. Nigam S.R., Local Government, S. Chand and Company, New Delhi-1982.

27. Ommen, M. A., "Fiscal decentralization in Kerla, in Geeta Sethi (ed), Fiscal Decentralization to Rural Government in India, Oxford University Press, 2004.

28. Rau M.G. and Singh Nirvikar, Political Economy of Federalism in India, Oxford University Press, 2005.

29. Sinha, Anil Kumar, Bihar Panchayat Raj : Vidhi Aur Vidhan, Estern Book Agency, Patna, 2006.

30. Sinha Anugrah Narain, मेरे संस्मरण, Reprint, Kusum Prakashan, Patna-1960.

31. Sarswati Swami Sahjanand, मेरा जीवन संघर्ष, Sitaram Ashram, Bihta, Patna-1952.

32. Srivaram Krishana K.K. Court, Panchayats and Nagarpalikas, Background and review of the Case law, Academic Fundation, New Delhi.

33. Vallan Court Francies and M. Richard Bird: Fiscal Decentralization in Developing Countries, Cambridge University Press, Cambridge, 1998.

34. Sharma B.K., Additional Seceretary- Government of India, Bharat Ka Samvidhan, 1 Nov 1998., New Delhi.

B. Journals, Articles and Book Chapters

1. De Indarani, Economic and Political Weekly, Can Decentralization Improve, Rural Water Supply Service, Jan-2009.

2. Radu Ban, et.al., The Political Economy Village Sanitation in South India (Policy Research Working Paper) World Bank, December-2008.

3. Mehrotra Nillka & S. M. Patnaik, October 25, 2008 *Economic and Political Weekly*, Culture versus Coercion, other side of Nirmal Gram Yojana.

4. Mathew George and B.S. Baviskar, Inclusion and exclusion in local governance, Sage Publications, New Delhi-2009.

5. Magdalana, Karl-oskar lindgren, Inkinen, Sten widmain: Who Knows best what the people want; women or man? A study of Political Representation in India, Comparative Political Studies, Vol-42, No-1.

6. Mishra Soumya, Savvy: et.al. Searching for Rights: Reality Check, Down to Earth, 1-15 July 2008. Economic and Political Weekly, March-11-17, 2006 Vol-XLI, No.10.

7. M.A. Ommen –Fiscal Decentralization to Sub-State Level Governments, Economic and Political Weekly, Vol. 41 (10), March 11, 2006. pp. 897-903.

8. Mahsbridge Jane: "Does Participation make better citizens"? The Good Society-5.2. (Spring) 1995 PP 1-7.

9. Heller Patrick : (Democratic Deepening in India and South Africa) Journal of Asian and African Studies, Vol-44 - No.1.

10. Kumari A Santhi:- Overview of Andhra Pradesh Smart Card Project, Kurukshetra, January, 2009.
11. Panchayat Update, Institute of Social Sciences, New Delhi.
12. Ray Sthitatragyan: Alleviating Proverty through Micro-Finance: SGSY, Experience in Orissa, Sociological Bulletin, May, 2008.
13. Rao, Vijayendra, Raduban:- Tokenism or Agency? The impact of Women's Reservation on village Democracies in South India, Economic and Cultural Change, April 2008.
14. Roy Ramashray, Gandhi Soundins in Political Philosophy, Chanakya Publication, Delhi, 1984.
15. Singh Panbir. Strengthening Panchayat, The Tribune 20 April, 2008.
16. Rajaraman Indira and Darshy Sinha, Functional Devolution to Rural Local Bodies in Four States, Economic and Political Weekly, 42124, 16 June 2007, pp. 2275 to 2283.
17. Tiwari Nupur and Acyara Manishankar : Inclusive Growth through Inclusive Governance of India, Journal of Local Governance, January, 2009.
18. Vanaik Anish Sidhartha : CAG Report on NAREGA : Fact and Fiction, Economic and Political Weekly, 21-27 June, 2008.
19. Whalen Hugh : Ideology, Democracy and the Foundations of Local Self-Government, Methuen Toronto, 1970.
20. Ministry of Panchayati Raj. New Delhi; State of Panchayats; 2007-08 (Three Volumes).
21. Datta, Abhijit, Strengthening Panchayat Finance : A New Approach, Indian Institute of Public Administration, New Delhi, April 2009, pp. 1-25.
22. Bhandari, Laveesh and VN Alok, Rating the Policy and Functional Environment of PRIs in Different States of India - A Concept Paper, Indian Institute of Public Administration, New Delhi, May 2009, pp. 1-11.

23. Roy, Ash Narain, Local Government in 2008, Institute of Social Sciences, New Delhi, 2009, pp. 1-3.

24. Moolakkattu, John, Some Problems in Measuring the Decentralisation of Political Power, Loyala Journal of Social Science, Vol. 23, No. 1, Jan-June 2009, pp. 1-17.

25. Alok, V. N., 'Share of Local Governments in the Union Divissible Pool : An Option's submitted to V. Ramchandran - led Expert Group, 2006, pp. 1-23.

Index